The Exit

How to sell your weird bootstrapped niche tech business

The full story (in unnecessary detail) of a seven-figure exit by a solo founder for a bootstrapped SaaS business—start to finish.

(A guide for founders who have no idea what they're doing)

The Exit: How to sell your weird bootstrapped niche tech business

First published in the United States in 2026.

ISBN 978-1957452258

No artificial intelligence was used in the design or composition of this book.

For information, bulk requests, or general inquiries, please contact:

peter@peteryoung.me

Dedicated to those who refused to surrender.

Contents

ACT ONE

THE GROUNDWORK

Several years ago I sold my weird bootstrapped SaaS business for a "multiple seven figure" amount. Not enough to get an Epstein intro (he was dead), enough to never have to work again.

I'm sharing the entire process of selling your weird solo-founder tech (or non-tech) business for millions when you have no mentors, and no idea what you're doing (I was both).

If you're a solo, non-tech founder who is selling a smaller (seven-figure ARR) bootstrapped SaaS business (as I was), this story will be most instructive. If you don't check all those boxes, this will still have value.

Today, the wealthy (vs. merely rich) would disparagingly call me a "single digit millionaire." But prior to my late-start "success," I banked over 15 years of adulthood where I was happily broke and did nothing but accumulate stories. Then, I spent six years running an extremely profitable business where most profit went right into my pocket. Even before my exit, I was ahead of most.

If you don't want to read about my twisted, rogue, and occasionally illegal path to financial freedom, you can skip ahead. But the TL,DR is: No college degree. No family money. Almost no work experience. And I went from nearly-destitute to retired in six years.

What you're going to get from this

- Everything you should do to prepare to sell your business.
- What I should have done, but didn't.
- How to get a broker to sell your business.
- My pitch deck, slide by slide.
- What prospective buyers want to know.
- A bunch of stories about funny and/or terrifying things that happened during the process.
- My top mistakes (that cost me millions).
- Everything that reduced my business valuation (don't do these).
- Tons of actionable lessons and weird minutiae that no one else talks about.

You'll come away knowing that as unsure you are about whether you're "doing things right," there's someone who's done things even less-right.

Teaser: In addition to all of the above, I'll be sharing one specific mistake that cost me seven figures, and another one that cost me six. You can use these for a laugh, as anti-instructional, or both.

Why this is different from other "I sold my startup" stories

Before selling my SaaS business, I watched a bunch of videos and read a few books, and I found a several things missing:

Everything was clinical and how-to. I never found a detailed personal narrative on the whole process, start to finish. Something that included all the weird decisions and emotional turbulence of the process.

Little was relevant to my specific situation. Lots of "micro acquisition" (six figure) stories. And many eight and nine figure ones. And many seven-figure exits that involved investors or co-founders. Very little from solo founders in the seven-figure ARR no-man's land—for whom a seven-figure exit will be life changing (and they get to keep all the money).

It all felt sanitized of guilt, shame, or uncertainty. No one wanted to admit they entered the process clueless, marched into the abyss, found themselves in a tornado of uncertainty and difficult decisions, fumbled their way through it, and came out the other side only partially victorious—a victory subdued by mistakes and regrets.

They left many unanswered questions. How do taxes work? What can derail a sale? Are there reasons to accept the non-highest offer? What happens after the sale? Is everything really as linear as depicted?

In this story, I'm telling the *whole* story, with a level of detail that will be offensive to anyone of literary pedigree. Along with the megadose of detail, you get a megadose of honesty—what I did wrong, how I thought through challenging decisions, and how my cluelessness (probably) cost me multiple seven-figures.

Who this is for (and not for)

<u>Most relevant</u>: You're a first-time, solo, non-tech founder of a bootstrapped SaaS company with seven-figure ARR.

<u>Very relevant</u>: You're a first-time, solo, founder of a bootstrapped tech company.

<u>Still relevant</u>: You're a founder of anything, looking to sell.

What this story is *not*

This book is 80% what happened to me, 20% what I've "researched." And neither the 80% nor the 20% covers everything.

I will not exhaustively turn over every stone of exiting a business. Instead, this documents my first hand experience of selling a specific kind of business, of a specific size, with some specific challenges (and advantages).

This is largely limited to experiences I personally faced, interspersed with knowledge I researched enough to credibly share, or knowledge personally conveyed to me by experts.

I didn't face every possible obstacle. I faced bigger decisions than a smaller business, and smaller decisions than a bigger business.

You'll find other books and articles that cover exits, yet no one is going into all the emotional turbulence and weird edge case decision making they went through in this level of detail. Only someone as autistic as me would overshare this level of minutiae.

While I've only had one exit (so far), I'm confident no two are alike. I hope this story offers some comfort that whatever weird impasses, grievous errors, or regrettable sacrifices you experience on the way to the finish line—you're not the only one. By exposing the reader to the sheer variety of weirdness I went through, I hope to convey that whatever weirdness you experience is not that weird.

(You're encouraged to supplement with more exhaustive resources so you're fully armed for battle. I found Selling Your Software Company by Dave Kauppi to be a great one.)

Pre-requisites

This is not written for voyeurs, and it's not written to entertain. If you're reading, I'm assuming the following:

- You have a business.
- Your business is profitable or has some assets of value.
- Your business is sellable (it can theoretically be run without you).

ACT TWO

THE ORIGIN STORY

A brief history of me having no idea what I'm doing

If you're like me, you read stories like this and think—"this isn't relevant to me because XYZ doesn't apply." So allow me to explain how I represent the most unlikely person to sell anything for seven figures (i.e. if I can do it, literally anyone can).

My childhood was flatly middle class. Most of it was spent in affluent towns we really couldn't afford. This early exposure to "success" may have conferred some advantages I haven't fully identified, but I already digress. Assuredly, I'm not downplaying anything for peasant-cred when I say: My family did not have money.

At 18, I made the declaration I would never have a job for the rest of my life. Many declarations made at this age aren't honored, but I was committed to this one. To date I have been employed less than 18 months of my adult life.

This "militant unemployment" journey began with living in abandoned houses (the first, located at: 2221 66th Ave SE, Mercer Island, WA), I dumpster dived and shoplifted my food, and lived on under $2 a day. Not for a summer, but for seven years.

At 25 I experienced my first lifestyle upgrade, refining an illicit side hustle (not drugs) which funded an apartment near the beach in Santa Cruz, California.

At 27 I went to prison on federal "eco-terrorism" charges for releasing thousands of mink from fur farms (where they raise them to make fur coats). If you're wondering, I have no regrets about this.

At 29 I was released and forced to "go straight," when I had no idea what that looked like. Specifically, this took the form of cheap rooms in friends homes, and a patchwork of revenue streams as small as they were inconsistent.

At 33 I seized upon my first consistent, legal business endeavor: Selling used books on Amazon.

At 34, I enjoyed my first year with income that could be considered "middle class." And just kidding, I didn't enjoy it—it was terrible (worse than poor).

At 35 I declared an end to the middle class experiment, and decided that only 1. The rich and 2. The poor are truly free. I committed myself to make a Hail Mary attempt at #1, and return to #2 if that didn't work.

At 36 I snuck into a $3,500 conference where two speakers gave a presentation about "software as a service" (SaaS) as the "ultimate freedom business." Desperate, in a "running out of time" way, I signed up for their course. Cost: about 20% of my net worth.

At 37 I hired a developer and launched my SaaS business. Despite having no idea what I was doing, the business peaked at $2.2 million revenue.

Six years after launch, I sold the business and retired.

Everything that follows is about that last part: The process of selling your business for millions when you've made every mistake.

Stumbling towards "success"

If the timeline I just shared didn't oversell my point, I'll do it here: There was (almost) no one whose life set him up for failure more than me.

My 20s were a zero-regrets tornado of unconventional travel (hitchhiking, hopping freight trains, roadying for punk bands), unconventional living situations (not just abandoned houses but abandoned boats, stairwells of college libraries, prison), and generally optimizing for stories and experiences (and certainly not "the future.")

My early 30s were the same, with less homelessness and fewer arrestable offenses, but an equal level of disregard for "where all this was going." I entered my mid-30s an un(formally)-educated felon who had worked less than 18 months of his adult life. Not only did I have no resume, I was flatly unwilling to be unemployed. I'd come this far, and I wasn't going to sell out now.

By mid-30s, I noticed everyone in my age bracket was in either an SSRI or W2 zombie state (usually both). That's when the whole "reality" thing hit. Feeling out of time, I plotted a desperate move where I would set myself up to eliminate the threat of ever having to be employed. I.e. I wanted a financial windfall and early retirement (I know, me and everyone else).

To buy myself time, I sold used books on Amazon. Meanwhile, I deep-dove into various internet business models to pull off my Grand Exit. This journey culminated in forging a pass to an aforementioned $3,500 conference (sorry organizers, I plead desperation) and being introduced to the "Software As A Service" (SaaS) model.

With the money I'd saved from reselling used books (much of them sourced from midnight raids on library dumpsters), I hired a developer and spent $14,000 on my first SaaS—a niche tool for a niche market to profit from a non-niche ecommerce site in a very niche way.

Now 37, with a significant percentage of my life savings tied up, this wasn't a "fingers crossed" experiment. I was (almost) out of time, and (almost) out of money. This *had* to work.

On launch day, I had 100 users at $97 a month.

Six months later, I was doing $30k a month.

Revenue hovered at $40k a month for three years.

With organic growth and no advertising costs, I did something every MBA would consider sacrilegious: I put every dollar that came in right into my pocket. No "reinvesting in the business." That was for adults with business acumen. I, on the other hand, had no such confidence. Certain everything would collapse the next day, I pocketed every dollar.

Around year three I became a cash-millionaire.

Four months after that, my net worth hit $1.3 million liquid *and* a paid-for house (money does not move linearly).

The business peaked at $120k a month.

After building out upsells and one-time offers, I had two consecutive years of $2 million+ revenue.

In year six the business had trended down to $100k a month, and I could see the way the wind was blowing. I had reached the limits of how far a 2.5 person team (me, a dev, and a part-time support person) could take this.

Time for my Grand Exit.

That's where this story really begins.

A few disclaimers (legal and otherwise)

Two things I can't/shouldn't/won't reveal in this story:

I avoid sharing the exact terms of my exit *(including selling price)*. My asset purchase agreement has a ton of legalese I don't really want to untangle and it's not entirely clear what specifics shouldn't be publicized. *"Ok so run the contract through AI or just ask your lawyer and tell us everything?"* I could but I don't care that much. It was a "multi seven figure amount." Use your imagination.

I avoid naming the business. This is for a very different reason. I used a pseudonym for all public-facing parts of the business due to the colorful Google footprint of my real one *(see: my criminal history, earlier this chapter)*. Today, I have no active business dealings in the specific market where I built the business, but maybe I will again one day. Better to keep my options open. Would anyone care if the founder of a tool they use had a 20+ year old criminal record for freeing mink? Probably not, but there's no upside either, so better to keep the business anon. In fact, every entrepreneur should use a pseudonym. Why wouldn't you? I think it's weird not to.

This is what my business looked like at the time I sold

- Super-niche SaaS tool that facilitated a super niche business model.

- $100,000 MRR
- Six years old.
- Solo non-tech founder.
- $0 customer acquisition cost / 100% organic, inbound marketing.
- Two employees (one dev, one part-time customer support)
- $97 / month or $997 / year for the primary offer.
- A half-dozen paid add on Chrome extensions, premium version, various upsells.
- Bad churn.
- Run as a cash-flow, lifestyle business.

That covers the basics.

My SaaS tool was in the "make money online" niche (which will factor heavily into the outcome of this story). It aggregated a mountain of data from a very large ecommerce platform, organized it in a specific way, made it sortable, and helped users identify opportunities to profit ("buy low, sell high"). Users also received an in-depth course on using the tool for maximum profits. For $97/month, users got access to "tools, training, and community."

The journey we're about to cover

Here's the journey I'm documenting, from deciding to exit, to the close:

- Making the decision to sell.

- The prep work required to get ready: From tax prep to dressing up my skeletons to getting everything ready for a new owner.
- Making a pitch deck.
- Getting a lawyer.
- Finding an M&A broker.
- Going to market.
- Finding a buyer.
- The "Letter of Intent."
- Due diligence.
- The Asset Purchase Agreement.
- Navigating negotiations.
- The close.
- Onboarding new owners.

And more instructional hilarity and unforgivable crimes that will be revealed throughout.

Before I sold, everything was a mess

The $100k MRR was the only impressive part of the entire business.

From launch until sale, I was in way over my head. The only aspects of the business I was competent in were copywriting and sales. Put one of my emails,in a prospects inbox, and they were in imminent risk of being converted. Put them on one of my live webinars, and they're as good as sold. Apparently you can build a seven-figure business being good at those two things and nothing else. Because every other part of my business was a disaster.

I never figured out how to hire well. The entire operations side was chaos. I spent 30 minutes a day searching for random files because nothing was organized. I had no bookkeeper. I probably overpaid on taxes. And so on.

My greatest crime (in the eyes of anyone with business acumen) is how little I understood the importance of reinvesting revenue in the business, to increase its value for an eventual sale. From day one, I operated under the belief the whole business was going to implode any day. So every dollar that came in above operating expenses went right into my pocket.

That means no paid ads. No affiliate outreach. No sales team. Just content marketing (barely) and paying some outrageous tax rate on all profits that went straight to my personal account. My whole attitude was, "I live on $5k a month. I'm bringing in $100k a month. Getting to $150k a month doesn't move the needle on my life." Pure cash flow business. There was always the intent to sell, but never a timeline or "plan."

I operated with a level of paranoia that may or may not have been justified, believing the business was "too good to be true" and couldn't last. Threats of changes to the *<the unnamed ecommerce platform>* Terms of Service . Concerns about third party API dependency. Increasing competition. And so on.

Today I understand that increasing your business valuation is the highest ROI move you can make. That most "set for life" money doesn't come from the revenue you pull out of the business along the way—the real payday happens when you sell.

I now understand better that keeping money in the business would have had a multiplying effect, and could have condensed a six year journey into a three year journey – and for a much bigger payday.

This isn't an article on how to run your business, but it is an article on everything I did both right and wrong over the course of selling mine. Had one of those aforementioned Very Bad Things I was paranoid about actually happened, and had the business collapsed, taking profits ensured I'd walk away with something. And I would look back on that decision as wise insurance.

In light of what actually happened, putting that money into ads or something would have meant a deferred, but much larger, payday. My seven figure exit could have been eight.

Yes, this is obvious to most. All I'm saying is, I had no idea what I was doing…

Making the decision to sell

The decision for me was very easy, and I didn't struggle with it at all.

Four circumstances converged to make my decision to sell one of high conviction:

My developer was leaving. He had been with me for most of the life of the business, and was leaving. While he was theoretically replaceable, I was starting down a high-stakes hiring process as someone who was as good at hiring as being an employee (i.e. not good).

I was in an innovation stalemate. I'd just had my two biggest years, revenue-wise. At the same time, I had decreasing confidence I could maintain my current revenue without introducing new products. And I was simply out of new ideas.

I was unwilling to scale. I had entered that low seven-figure revenue No Man's Land, where doubling the business means quadrupling your expenses (paid ads, hiring, etc), leaving your net profit no better for the effort. Scaling up would require the next level of complexity, without the next level of profit. And I just wasn't willing to go there.

Honeymoon phase was over. Like relationships, I was approaching that seven year mark where you just emotionally check out.

It was time.

If the decision for you isn't so simple, I'll just pass along a sentiment that came up over and over as I researched other founder's stories, and how they wrestled with this question:

"If you have to ask if it's time to sell, you know the answer."

Again, kind of like relationships.

Then I received an unsolicited offer

After mentioning my vague plans to exit the business to a couple friends, I got on the radar of someone with deep pockets.

You should never take the first offer that comes along (some exceptions may apply—hold that thought), but I agreed to take his call.

After probing my business, then pitching me on his credentials and other businesses he'd acquired and grown, he made an immediate offer of $2 million.

Even with my cursory knowledge of business valuation, I knew it was a ridiculous and predatory offer. My answer was a hard no, but having an offer did serve the role of shifting me into a new mode: *I was now a man with a business for sale.*

ACT THREE

PREPPING FOR THE SALE

Laying the Groundwork: Everything I did before the sale

Biography over. So you've decided to sell. Here's how I did it...

This is not a car. You don't toss the keys to a new owner. Significant prep work is involved.

The importance of all these preamble details cannot be overstated. None of it is fun, but—since this may be the biggest financial event of your life—all it worth focusing on.

One mantra to chant here is:

"The Confused Mind Always Says No."

Or perhaps,

"The Risk Averse Mind Sees Risk And Says No."

Nearly everything you're going to do from this point is directly related to buyer psychology.

Everything that gives a potential buyer pause, anything that is inconsistent, and anything that makes them confused; translates as risk.

And for buyers, risks are either priced in, or avoided.

Prepping your business means:

- Knowing (and having) all documentation a buyer needs.
- Presenting a clear, transparent financial backstory.
- Having a clear road map for growth.
- Minimizing risks for new owners.
- Reducing all operational and cognitive friction to new ownership.
- Maximizing valuation.

This is the time to start getting the house ready for guests (and their money). Here's everything I did…

#1 Determining if I had a sellable business

Many entrepreneurs believe having revenue makes their business inherently sellable. In fact, there's many reasons your business could be less-than-appetizing from an acquisition standpoint.

A common scenario is founders operating their business as a "lifestyle business," where they operate lean, and are involved in everything. Then it comes time to sell and no one wants to buy because their business will collapse if the founder isn't involved. It wasn't built with the end in mind.

Another scenario is a business with healthy revenue but encumbered with liabilities. Whether debt, litigation, threat of regulatory headwinds, or other red flags. Cash flow isn't always enough.

First step is to determine if you have a business anyone wants. If your business is toxic from an acquisition standpoint, you have work to do.

The SaaS model—with its scalability and recurring revenue—was known to be a desirable model for acquiring entities. That was where my confidence ended.

Everything else—valuation, fatal flaws in my metrics, etc—was a question mark.

#2: Making my business as turnkey as possible

In short: I created manuals, tutorials, and SOPs for everything.

The goal here is to dummyproof your business so new owners can throw an intern into the fray and they'd be able to operate without total collapse.

The more buyers think you're a linchpin, the lower they're interest. This is a point beaten into your head by entrepreneur starter pack books like the *E Myth*, but if you've never read those, you need to hear this:

If your business can't run without you, no one will buy it.

So list out everything you do on a day to day basis, and turn it into an SOP, text tutorial or video.

A few of the documents I created:

- How to use my software.
- Managing the support inbox.
- How to manage cancellation requests.
- Paying affiliates.
- How to moderate live webinars.
- Refund request protocols.

And many more.

Make the onboarding of a new owner and team as frictionless as possible, and increase your appeal to buyers.

#3 Documenting my code base

Just kidding, I didn't do this. And it's actually insane I got away with it.

When I told my lead developer to prep for a near-future sale, he told me, in so many words, documenting his code on short notice was not possible. It was too big, he said. No one can do it but me, he said. And we don't have enough time, he said.

Entirely possible this detail could have cost me a sale. Do not follow my lead here: If you're selling a tech business, document your code base.

#4 Getting my face off the business as much as possible

Here's another one I didn't do. And it probably hurt my valuation.

Selling a business is like inviting cops into a crime scene. And the first thing any guilty criminal does in a crime investigation is "minimize their involvement." This criminal is you. The "crime" is your business. And your job is to minimize your involvement.

The more your face or name is associated with the business, the less confident a buyer will be that success can be maintained when you're gone. That personal touch you bring may be your business's greatest asset, but it can become its greatest liability at the time of a sale.

When it came time to sell, my successors were explicit they viewed my business as "guru lead," and valued it accordingly. This was not a good thing.

Selling a business that only works because there's a dancing monkey "guru" on its face can be toxic to buyers. This can bring your valuation down from an 8x or 10x multiple to a 2x or 3x.

Obviously don't conceal crucial facts. If your business is guru-lead, it is what it is. And for some businesses, it's simply not possible to downplay.

But this might be a good time to remove your personal bio from the sales page, take your name off the YouTube channel, depersonalize your onboarding email sequence, and generally "minimize your involvement."

#5 Cleaning up my books

Another "selling your business 101" thing, but a big one. If your accounting records are anything other than impeccable, buyers will see risk and uncertainty.

Even if your books are in perfect order, find a service that will optimize your financials *specifically* for a sale. I learned in this process that there are ways to organize your books to make them more appetizing to a buyer than the "normal" way.

This "acquisition optimized" way to rearrange your records is not dishonest. There's nothing concealed or manipulated. But there are ways to organize a P&L and balance sheet that look better to possible acquirers. Sort of the financial equivalent of photographers understanding your best angles.

I used a company called CapForge. There are countless others.

There's almost no expense that isn't justified when you're prepping for a sale, but this one is near the top.

#6 Cleaning up my house of weird, shady stuff

Every business has skeletons. (Or is it just mine?)

These skeletons can take many forms.

Does your sales page have a ton of stolen IP? I made liberal use of Google Images on mine. I also didn't bother to clean that up. But probably should have.

Are you doing some shady, gray hat stuff under the hood of your tech business? Time to see if there's a less offensive way to accomplish the same thing.

One of our add-on tools (separate from the primary offer) was scraping data from a major site—one that perhaps would prefer we weren't doing that. There was no alternate way to get this data, and I was transparent about it. This ended up not being a concern for the buyer, but maybe should have been (a few years after the sale, our scraping methodology stopped working).

Does your business have training material featuring an interview with someone outside the company? Do you have a release form for this content?

Have you violated the Geneva Convention of business competition and engaged in an online smear campaign against a competitor? Could a buyer see this as a legal (or reputational) liability?

It's not just one person or executive team who will make the decision to acquire your business. It may require lawyer approval, accountant approval, dev lead approval, *and* executive approval. If you raise alarms among any of them, it could kill the deal.

Look at your business with fresh eyes, consider anything an owner, accountant, or lawyer could object to, and clean up house.

#7 Installing website analytics

This won't apply to 995/1,000 people. The other 5/1,000 are as incompetent as I (almost) was.

I say "almost" because I *almost* didn't have any web analytics installed. And if I'd skipped this, it might have cost me the sale.

Who doesn't at least have Google Analytics installed? Almost no one, but it's my duty to inform you that you must be able to prove website traffic and sources before putting your business up for sale.

Jumping ahead: when we arrived at the "due diligence" phase of the sale, the counterparty naturally wanted to know my traffic sources. When I couldn't answer that question on a live call with any specificity, they were suspicious, indignant, and indirectly accused me of a cover up. I only talked them down by giving them access to my Google Analytics account.

It was only by luck that I had installed it several years before. It's possible I'd never even looked at it. Had the buyers not had this transparency into my sales page traffic sources, it is possible the sale would not have closed. (That was a heated call.)

#8 Cleaning up my online presence

If you have negative reviews, hater-chatter, or anything that reflects poorly on you or your business, you probably don't have any control over it.

But to the extent that you might, this would be a time to extend some olive branches and work to have anything bad taken down.

Going into the sale, I had a few online blemishes. One blog post with an unfavorable review that declared a competitor better. One YouTube comparison review from the same person. And one weird Youtube review with <100 views from a guy in a thick accent of unknown origin who clearly didn't understand my tool at all.

I had decisive plans to get the blog/Video #1 guy on the phone and bribe my way into making those hit pieces vanish. But miraculously, through no effort of my own, the guy erased his entire online presence shortly before the sale. Two down, one to go.

With Video #2, it was anonymous, his review was easy to debunk, there was nothing I could do about it anyway, and in the end it didn't matter.

#9 Thoroughly removing anything personal from the business

Most "real" businesses run by "real" entrepreneurs (those with business acumen) will be unlikely to have this problem. I, on the other hand, had work to do.

In preparing for a future where you hand over the keys to your castle, ensure there are no personal effects left behind.

Probably the worst mistake in this category is commingling finances. Such as personal funds and business funds sharing the same bank account. (Worse than problematic for a sale, this could also be a legal issue. I'm not a cop. I'm just saying.)

Fortunately, my business wasn't that chaotic. But I did commingle everything that *wasn't* money. For example, over the six years I ran the business, I was easier to reach via my "support@" business email than my personal email. Sometimes even more so than my phone. This was clear to anyone who knew me, and my support inbox was probably 2% personal email. This had to be remedied before total strangers had ownership of the inbox. It took me half a day to delete everything.

Likewise I had tons of personal files mixed up in business folders. All of it had to be sorted.

#10 Getting all my papers together

This is a general battlecry to both gather and organize all crucial documents an acquiring party may ask for.

If you had an offer tomorrow, would you have all the documents a buyer will request to both audit and operate your business?

I'm referring to:

- Corporate bylaws
- Employee records and contracts
- Articles of incorporation
- Correspondence with local, state ,or federal governments pertaining to your business
- Licenses or permits needed to operate the business
- Federal or local tax correspondence: audits, notices, etc
- Non-compete agreements
- Non-disclosure agreements
- All contracts with consultants, contractors, customers or vendors
- All litigation or legal records
- Anyone who owns a stake in the business and accompanying shareholder agreements, stock certificates, etc
- Loan documents
- Three to five years of financials (balance sheets, profit and loss statements, etc)
- Bank statements

- Three to five years of tax returns

…and more.

All of these should exist, and be organized.

Before a sale closes, you'll be asked to produce dozens (or hundreds) of documents, often on short notice, and you need to have everything together.

#11 Getting intimate with my metrics (and getting a second opinion on all of them)

The quantitative side of your business is going to do most of the heavy lifting in a sale. And I'm a great example of how far you can get without knowing anything.

What follows is a list of the top metrics a buyer will want to know (and want proof of). I could not recite most of these (and couldn't even define some of them) prior to this process.

If you're using Stripe, you can get some of these from the dashboard. There are paid tools that can generate the rest. Or do it by hand, like I did.

Here are the top 10 metrics a buyer will want to know (if you're selling a tech business):

1. Monthly Recurring Revenue (MRR)
2. Net Revenue Retention

3. Gross Revenue Retention
4. Customer Churn Rate
5. Revenue Growth Rate
6. Gross Margin
7. Customer Acquisition Cost (CAC)
8. LTV / CAC Ratio Measures unit economics and long-term value creation
9. EBITDA
10. Customer Concentration: % of revenue from top 1, 5, or 10 customers (High concentration = higher perceived risk)

Two final warnings I feel strongly about because I learned the hard way:

1. Get a second opinion on all metrics. Sign up for multiple SaaS metrics tools, look for discrepancies (they are inevitable), and pick the one that seems most accurate (or just pick the best one and take your chances).
2. Audit each one for inaccuracies. I calculated one of these incorrectly for my pitch deck. And I believe it was a seven-figure mistake. More on that later.

#12 Mapping out a growth plan

For me, this was the only prep work I found fun.

Your growth plan is where you sell the potential of what your business could become under new ownership.

My plan was amazing, and came together almost effortlessly.

For six years I had spent most waking moments brainstorming how to grow the business. As a solo founder committed to a small team, bandwidth issues had prevented me from doing almost all of them.

My growth plan may have been amazing, but it's not exactly a flex to say you have an "amazing" growth plan—it is, after all, just a list of everything you *should* have done, but didn't. Yet from a buyer's perspective, a clear path to growth is a huge selling point.

For me, this was a simple copy-and-paste effort directly from a spreadsheet where I ranked growth opportunities in order of revenue impact. My plan contained everything from international expansion to affiliate outreach to expanding into new product categories. Together, it formed a convincing blueprint to 3x to 5x the business in under a year.

My growth plan gave buyers conservative estimates and a bulletproof roadmap to significant growth, with a clear understanding of the bottlenecks that prevented this growth up to this point (*"I operate as a lifestyle business with an emphasis on cash flow over growth"* was how I explained most company deficiencies.)

Sell the vision of a much larger business and sell the dummyproof path to get there.

#13 Understanding taxes and minimizing my tax liability

This may be the part I spent the most time on, yet still understand the least. So a major disclaimer: I'm in no way qualified to offer guidance here. Only to share what I learned, lay out the concerns, as I understand them, and encourage you to hire a professional tax advisor knowledgeable in acquisitions (most aren't).

The IRS is going to get more of your sales price than your broker. And together, they're getting a big piece of the final pie. I'm going to tell you what I did to prepare, and what I didn't do but should have.

Three factors with the largest tax bill impact:

1. Is this an asset sale or a stock sale?
2. If an asset sale, which assets will be taxed as capital gains (lower rate) and which as income (higher rate)?
3. What is your tax election? (C-corp vs. anything else).

Massive disclaimer (again): I am not qualified to be advising on taxes. The implications of getting this wrong are huge. What follows is my limited understanding of taxes as it relates to selling your business—all of it gathered before I found an accountant and turned everything over to them.

Factor #1: Asset sale versus stock sale

An "asset sale" means a buyer is purchasing the assets of the business, not the business entity itself.

A "stock sale" means a buyer is purchasing ownership interests in the company, in the form of stock. The legal entity stays intact, along with its contracts, assets, and liabilities.

As a seller, you prefer a stock sale. You will pay less taxes.

A buyer prefers an asset sale. They will pay less taxes. And assume reduced liabilities.

If you're selling a business in the sub-$10 million range, asset sales are far more common. My M&A broker told me flatly he *never* handles sock sales.

You should petition for a stock sale whenever possible. But it may not be.

Factor #2: Capital assets vs non-capital assets

Assuming yours is an asset sale, estimating your tax liability is a matter of looking at all of the assets of the business (tangible and intangible) and determining which are **"capital assets"** and which are **"non-capital assets."**

The way to look at it is: your business is a collection of assets. Some of those assets are taxed as income (non-capital assets), and some of them are taxed at long term capital gains rate (capital assets). The greater the percentage of your business's value that you can argue (to the IRS) are capital assets, the lower your tax bill.

You can make a list of all assets in your business (anything that has value, from power point presentations to email lists), determine which fall into which category, then piece together an estimate of your tax burden.

This is where I also learned about "graduated long-term capital gains tax rates." You're taxed 0% on the portion of gains that falls below one threshold, 15% on the portion that falls in the middle range, and 20% on everything else. (These thresholds change, so I won't commit them to ink here. The general concept is likely to remain in place long term). Once I understood this, it brought my tax burden down from my initial estimates.

More good news: With the sale of a tech business, where most assets are intangible, the largest portion of value is made up of an asset called "goodwill." This is an intangible asset that covers things like the business's reputation, customer loyalty, etc. The value of the sale you assign to "goodwill" (in your state and federal tax reporting) is important because goodwill is taxed at a lower capital gains rate.

However there is a subjectivity to assigning value to various assets. If you sell your business for $5 million—what percentage of that $5m was paid for "goodwill" (taxed at a lower capital gains rate) and what percentage is the consulting value you offer the business after the close (taxed as income)? These are just two examples.

In a business like mine (SaaS), it is typical for more than 70% of the value to be assigned to goodwill. This was great news for my tax concerns.

Likewise, 10% of the value is typically assigned to the consulting agreement (any promise you make to a buyer to assist in growing or maintaining the business after the sale). And 5% is assigned to any non-compete agreement.

Assigning that value is subjective, but a tax expert familiar with acquisitions will understand the "standard" allotment (i.e. what won't trigger any alarms with the IRS).

Factor #3: Your tax election (and why it matters)

Specifically, how do you file with the IRS? There are various tax elections, but the main question to focus on here is: Do you file as a C-corp, or something else?

If you're engaged in an asset sale and file as a C-corp, contact a tax expert ASAP. This is a bad situation from a tax standpoint. I don't know what your options are, but I know that (as of this writing), you will be subject to double-taxation: Your corporation pays tax on asset sale, then you (as a shareholder) pay tax on the distribution. You urgently want to avoid this.

I filed as an S-corp. So I was fine. However the day I learned about the C-corp/S-corp tax implications, I spent a day having a drawn-out heart attack when I read that C-corps are double taxed. I had temporarily forgotten that S-corp election and C-corp election were different things, and thought that I would be giving up over half the sale proceeds to the IRS. That was a bad day.

(There's talk of undoing the "double taxation" impacting C-corps, but as of this writing it remains a threat.)

Bonus: Understanding "stock basis"

Of everything in this section, this is the one I understand least. It's borderline negligent for me to even be discussing it. But here it goes…

As I remember it, there are two ways to report expenses when filing your taxes. The typical way (the way I did it) is to report costs as expenses, then pay taxes on revenue minus those expenses. This minimizes taxes for the current year.

Filing with stock basis in mind means "capitalizing" costs that could be expensed. This increase tax bills in the short term, as you amortize expenses and create a "stock basis" for each asset in your business. But depending on your stock basis for each asset, your taxes are reduced at the time of sale—or not taxed at all.

As I was told by an accountant, amortizing expenses needs to be done years in advance for it to have an impact. If you're still years out from a sale, you can start now.

My journey trying to understand taxes

When "doing my own research" hit its limits, I hired a generic accountant to estimate my tax bill. They told me explicitly they were knowledgeable on this topic, could give me a number, and help me prepare. I realized very quickly they knew nothing, and fired them.

Then I hired a second firm who specifically advertised assisting business owners going through an acquisition. After providing them with a specific directive to analyze my business and provide me a specific number, the only thing they responded with was a generic spreadsheet to plug numbers into. I fired them too. (They still send me $5,000 invoices to this day and I will happily go to court over this. Clowns.)

It wasn't until my third attempt I received knowledgeable tax prep guidance, and a credible tax estimate. I was told my final bill would be somewhere between my best and worst case estimates (based on my solo research). This was something I could live with.

It was fortunate I had these questions answered early, because I learned your M&A broker is not going to help you. When I finally hired mine, I was surprised how little they knew about taxes, how little they cared, and how little interest they had in referring me to a tax planner. It's like how lawyers don't do anything to influence your prison designation (which I also have personal experience with). They don't know or care if you go to a minimum security or a maximum security. Anything after sentencing is not their concern.

As I understand it, the most apocalyptic tax scenario is selling a C-corp business (double taxed) where the assets are all tangible (taxed as income).

The takeaway is to find a good tax advisor knowledgeable in this specific area, and do it early.

#14 Deciding if I was willing to stay with the business

Your options to sell expand if you're willing to stay with the business after the sale. Whether as CEO, a lessor role, or just a long-term consultant.

You aren't likely to avoid *all* post-close labor. For most sales, a certain amount of knowledge transfer and migration help will be contractually required of you. You can't submit the final Docusign and immediately unplug and join an arctic expedition. That's not what I'm referring to by "staying with the business."

There are buyers who will only buy businesses if the owner stays with the company in a substantial role for an extended period.

Some founders are eager to get as far away from their business as possible. Others want to maintain their influence in the company, minus all the risk and boring parts.

You may have a *preference* about your involvement. But get clear about your *bottom line*. If a buyer is willing to walk away from a sale over your unwillingness to stay on as CEO, are you willing to kill the sale over this?

As for me, I had a strong preference to walk away completely. But my bottom line was a willingness to give 10 hours a week for a full year. Nothing more.

#15 Getting clear on my desired outcome

I feel strongly about this one. As I'll share later, not having an iron clad clarity of purpose almost cost me the sale when things momentarily went sideways.

What do I mean by "clarity of purpose"? Knowing exactly what outcome you're seeking in a sale. Not only a number, but the meaning behind the number. This is the outcome where, if the sale accomplishes it, you're happy.

Maybe you want to retire your parents. Maybe it's securing your dream property in Sun Valley. Maybe it's a vanity metric like "be a decamillionaire."

Whatever it is to you, have a clear outcome that determines if the sale was a "success." Something where, even if you sell for an amount far below your expectations, you can still be at peace with the result.

While I understood the value of being clear about my desired outcome, I didn't understand it well enough. That story will come later. But don't make my mistake.

My desired outcome was a number that ensured I could live well for the rest of my life if I never earned another penny.

I arrived at my number as a variation of something you may have heard of, called the "4% Rule." It goes like this: *"You will probably never run out of money if you can live for one year off 4% of your liquid net worth."* When they backtest this with a basic stock/bond portfolio allocation, for an average retirement length, the 4% rule works approximately 92% of the time.

Because my retirement would be over 20 years longer than average, I adjusted the 4% Rule to the 2.5% Rule. This means looking at my typical annual living expenses, then multiplied by 40 (making my expenses 2.5% of that number). Now I had my net worth target. If I received an offer where my proceeds (after taxes and broker fees) let me hit that number, then I would accept it.

That doesn't mean I would casually leave money on the table. Or allow myself to get robbed.

It meant if I would stop taking risks and creating friction at the exact point my outcome was guaranteed.

Having this clarity will give you a North Star when the sales process gets challenging, when you're being asked to give up things that are uncomfortable, when you're considering walking away, or when you're demanding things that could make the other side walk away.

RANDOM NOTES BEFORE TAKEOFF

Sell at the top (not when you're in a death spiral)

I chose to sell neither at the top, nor in a death spiral. However it's entirely possible that had I delayed a sale, revenue would have slipped into "death spiral" territory. And no one wants to be in a position of selling (or buying) a rapidly depreciating asset.

If you're like me, you didn't get serious about selling until it was semi-urgent. And you may not have the luxury of planning a sale 18 months out, allowing you time to stabilize or reverse declining numbers.

But $100k MRR that was $120k MRR yesterday is not the same as $100k MRR that was $80k MRR yesterday.

Sell at the top. Not when the ship is sinking.

Valuation: Understanding the basics

My advice: Go into the sales process understanding the broad strokes of valuation, while not being married to a number.

The market is going to speak, and you may not like what it says. But having some reference points may prevent you from getting totally robbed. (However your broker should safeguard against this more effectively.)

Let's say you're selling a B2B SaaS business. You'll read "most B2B SaaS sells at a 6x to 12x EBITDA multiple" (or whatever). Now you've anchored yourself on getting at least 6x, without being honest about all the ways these cookie cutter stats may not apply to your business at all.

Technically speaking I was running a B2B SaaS, and could have set myself up for wild expectations. But a closer look at my users revealed that for valuation purposes, it was more accurately a "micro-SMB SaaS." So now I was looking at a lower multiple. And that was before getting into any other blemishes or red flags. I was grateful I suffered from low-business-self-esteem and never had my heels dug in on an unrealistically high valuation.

By all means, look at comps if you can access this information. But you'll never know everything that drove their final price up or down.

Some would advise you to hire a valuation firm before going to market. I didn't, and relied on my M&A advisor.

There are many ways to value a business. If you want to take a (simplistic) shot at valuing yours, do this: Look at either your

SDE or EBITDA. Then decide on an appropriate multiple based on your business type.

Takeaway on valuation: Stay agnostic without being stupid.

Assembling your "exit team"

Here are the three professionals you need to hire before selling (after going through this, I would consider all three to be mandatory):

M&A broker *(or M&A advisor, for larger or more complex sales).* They will shop your business around and guide you through the whole process.

Accountant, CPA, or tax advisor
They will prepare your books for a sale, advise you on tax issues, and work to reduce your tax burden.

Attorney
Review contracts and navigate legal issues.

As an optional fourth, bring in a "valuation expert / appraiser" to set a realistic price.

Understand why businesses get acquired

There is a longer list of reasons business are acquired, but most fall into two categories:

1. **Financial**: A buyer sees a financial return based on current or potential revenue from the business.
2. **Strategic**: A buyer sees the potential to advance their current business strategy by acquiring yours. This covers a lot of motives, such as accessing a new customer base, eliminating you as competition, acquiring technology or intellectual property, and more.

In looking at my business, a financial acquisition seemed mostly likely. I occupied a weird niche, and wasn't perceived as a competitive threat to any much larger business who may want me for strategic reasons.

Listing out your direct competitors is recommended at this stage. While this was not useful in my case, these competitors are often the most eager to acquire you, and can be approached to get quick momentum.

ACT FOUR

FINDING AN M&A BROKER

Create a pitch deck

This is where I made a slide presentation – "*Here's my MRR, here's my ARPU, etc etc. Please buy me.*"

First thing I did was Google examples of pitch decks for SaaS businesses that had sold for seven or eight figures. Then I picked one mostly at random, and copied it.

Then I purchased a template I thought looked cool on Envato, and made the whole thing in Google slides.

Many might be tempted to embellish their numbers at this stage. Should go without saying, but starting now—there are no secrets. Everything will be laid bare. This isn't a dating app profile, where you can omit your felony record and hope they don't find out. (Bad example. I did omit my felony record from my deck and hoped they wouldn't find out, but this is a pitch deck not a dating profile). Point is: Everything is going to come out. The numbers are what they are, so either show your real ones, or retreat to improve them and come back in 12 to 18 months.

This process was uncomfortably vulnerable. For six years, I'd run my entire business in solitude. You never heard me on a business podcast or saw me blogging about my "entrepreneurial journey." Everything from my revenue to my metrics were completely private and had never been on display. Most of the metrics required for a pitch deck I didn't even know.

Here is a summary of every slide:

Slide #1: Sell the opportunity

Why waste time? Slide #1 simply read:

"<business name>: The opportunity. How a bootstrapped SaaS went to 7-figure net income with $0 customer acquisition cost (and how you can make it even better)"

Maybe I have PTSD from the time I tried (and failed) to shop a book proposal to literary agents, but I wanted to open with something that made advancing to the next slide irresistible.

Slide #2: Establish myself as the market leader

My SaaS pioneered a whole category. I made sure prospective buyers knew this on slide #2.

Slide #3: Problem / Solution

- What problem was my SaaS built to solve?
- How do we solve it better than anyone?

All of this was conveyed in four sentences.

Slide #4: Sell The Opportunity

My strategy was to make buyers think "this guy is an idiot and he's ignored tremendous growth potential." In fact this was my strategy for this entire process, from deck to purchase agreement.

This slide read:

"<business name> was launched as a lifestyle business, cash flow positive from day one.

A victim of its own success, it has outgrown its founder and original vision.

We have achieved 7-figures net income with no paid advertising, no sales team, $0 marketing budget."

Slide #5: High level snapshot

Five bullet points that explained:

- The platform. What kind of tool is this? In my case, a web-based tool with Chrome extension add-ons.
- The model: What is the revenue model? In my case, SaaS.
- The team: Who is running the show? I listed myself and my developer.
- The financials: How is it funded? In my case, bootstrapped.
- The tech stack: What languages and frameworks are used? In my case: Ruby On Rails, PostgreSQL, Sinatra, and Elasticsearch.

Slide #6: Historical timeline

Five bullet points highlighting milestones in the business:

From launch, to new revenue milestones, to the launch of other products or new features.

Slide #7: Pricing

The pricing scheme for my core product.

Slide #8: Pricing Part II

The pricing scheme for our Chrome extension add-ons.

Slide #9: The Big Numbers

Last year's net revenue and net income.

Slide #10: The Big Numbers, Part II

Current year's net revenue and net income.

Slide #11: MRR

Trailing three years of MRR, with a graph.

Slide #12: Paying Users

Trailing three years active user count, with a graph.

Slide #13: Trail-to-paid conversion

Last three years.

Slide #14: ARPU

Last three years, with a graph.

Slide #15: Customer LTV

Last three years, with a graph.

Slide #16: Asset list

What is everything a buyer gets with the sale?

I listed the following:

- Number of URLs.
- Number of sales funnels.
- Proprietary databases (we'd accumulated a mountain of historical pricing and sales data from the ecommerce platform our users sold on).
- "Goodwill" assets (we were the market originators, we had cred in the space, etc.)
- Marketing assets (our best converting assets were a 110-page physical book, and an automated webinar).
- Social media assets (a 4,000+ person private Facebook group).
- Email list (20,000 leads across various lists).
- Affiliate program.

That covered the basics.

Slide #17: Growth opportunities

I can't speak for buyers, but I considered this the most important slide. I put a lot of thought into every way a competent team could 3x the business in a short time.

Outlined were plans for high ticket sales, productizing our database with an API, international expansion, reducing churn, better affiliate outreach, and more.

I explained that the business side was run by one person (me) who simply didn't have the bandwidth.

All of this was explained briefly, but gave buyers a clear path to revenue growth.

Slide #18: Our markets

Who are our customers?

I wanted to give buyers a clear sense of who our customers were and why they used our product. I listed the "side hustle" market, "work from home" market, and two more.

Slide #19: Customer acquisition channels

I was utterly unforgivably stupid about not knowing how our users found us.

I put this into three buckets: organic traffic, content-driven traffic, and affiliates.

My hope was this slide got buyers with any marketing savvy salivating, because it painted the picture of me sleepwalking to $100k MRR.

Slide #20: User testimonials

I've truly never seen a SaaS testimonials page as glowing and voluminous as mine. My users were truly "raving fans." For this slide, I highlighted some of the best ones, and gave a link to the rest. This made it clear my tool delivered results.

Slide #21: Contact info

This one just read "Drive home safely" + email. I probably stole text verbatim from some other deck.

Done.

I had a deck I was confident would generate interest. It put the most compelling parts of the business forward, and saved the ugly parts for later (I would address those directly once I hooked some interest).

From the perspective of someone viewing my deck, I had a very sellable asset. Time to find a broker, and find out if I had something someone would pay millions for.

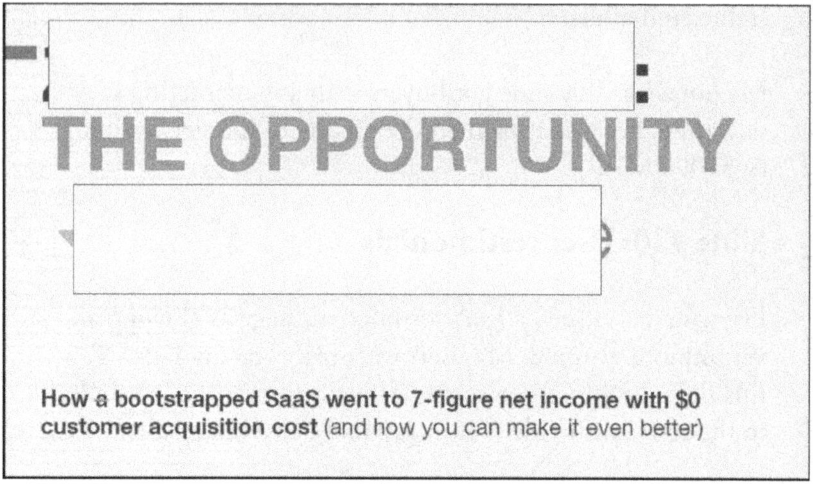
THE OPPORTUNITY
How a bootstrapped SaaS went to 7-figure net income with $0 customer acquisition cost (and how you can make it even better)

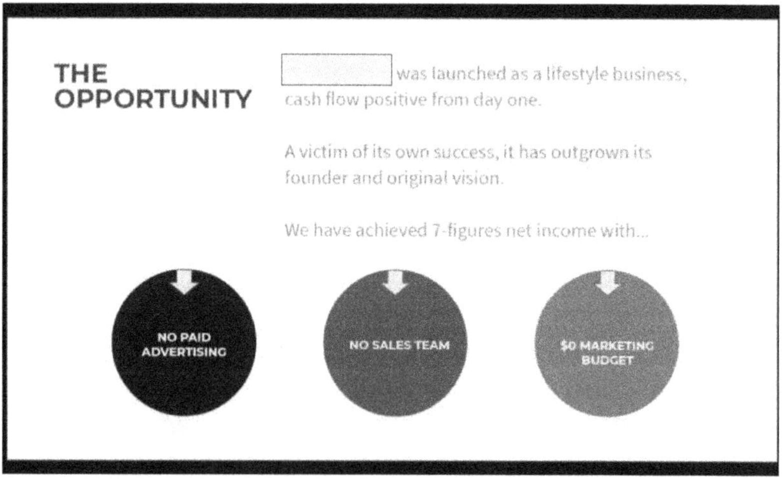
THE OPPORTUNITY
was launched as a lifestyle business, cash flow positive from day one.
A victim of its own success, it has outgrown its founder and original vision.
We have achieved 7-figures net income with...
NO PAID ADVERTISING
NO SALES TEAM
$0 MARKETING BUDGET

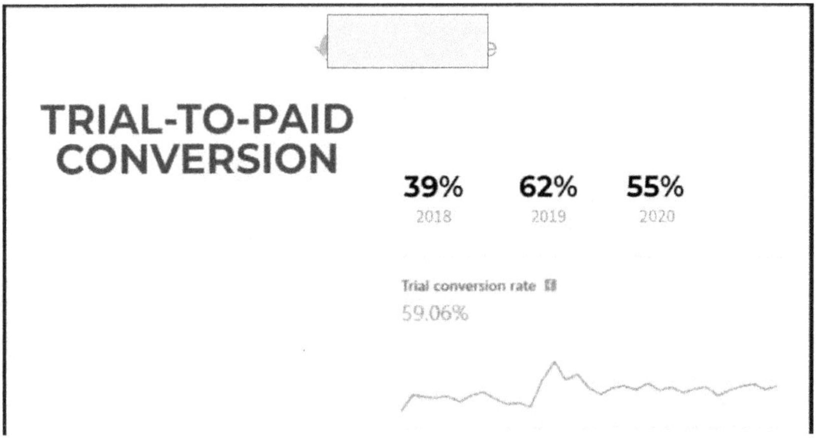
TRIAL-TO-PAID
CONVERSION
39%
2018
62%
2019
55%
2020
Trial conversion rate
59.06%

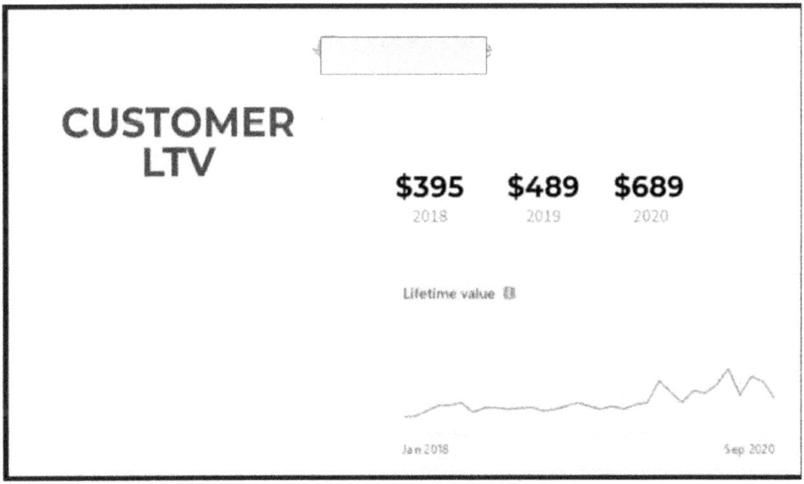
CUSTOMER
LTV
$395
2018
$489
2019
$689
2020
Lifetime value
Jan 2018
Sep 2020

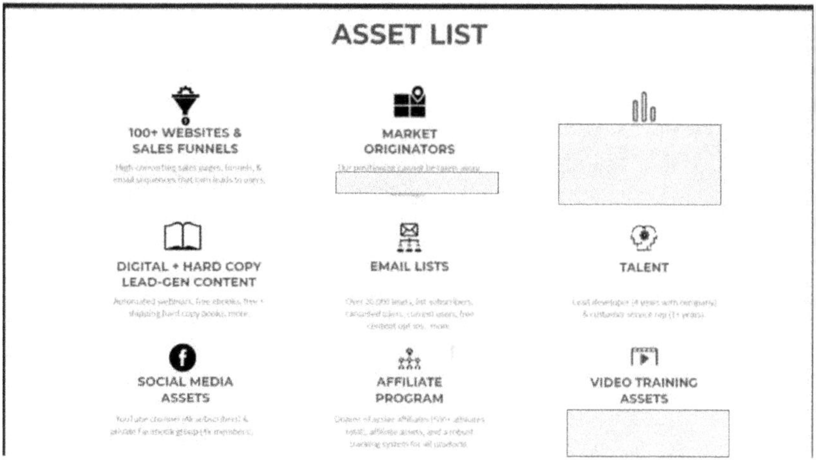
ASSET LIST
100+ WEBSITES & SALES FUNNELS
MARKET ORIGINATORS
DIGITAL + HARD COPY LEAD-GEN CONTENT
EMAIL LISTS
TALENT
SOCIAL MEDIA ASSETS
AFFILIATE PROGRAM
VIDEO TRAINING ASSETS

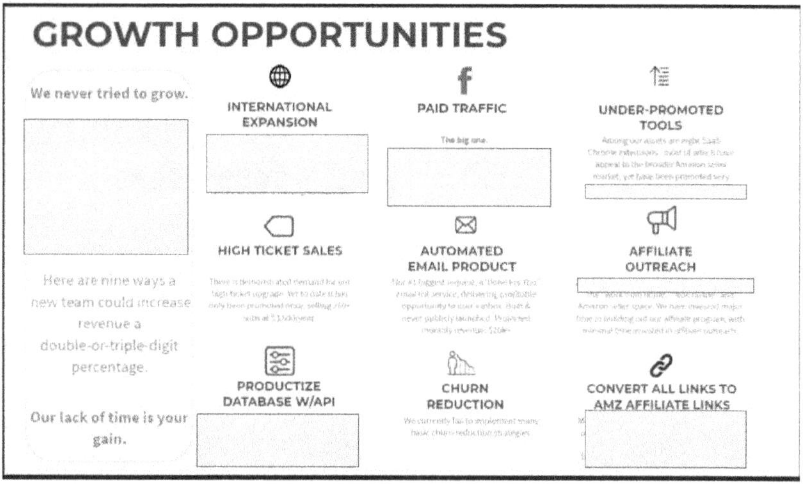
GROWTH OPPORTUNITIES
We never tried to grow.
INTERNATIONAL EXPANSION
PAID TRAFFIC
The big one.
UNDER-PROMOTED TOOLS
HIGH TICKET SALES
AUTOMATED EMAIL PRODUCT
AFFILIATE OUTREACH
Here are nine ways a new team could increase revenue a double-or-triple-digit percentage.
PRODUCTIZE DATABASE W/API
CHURN REDUCTION
CONVERT ALL LINKS TO AMZ AFFILIATE LINKS
Our lack of time is your gain.

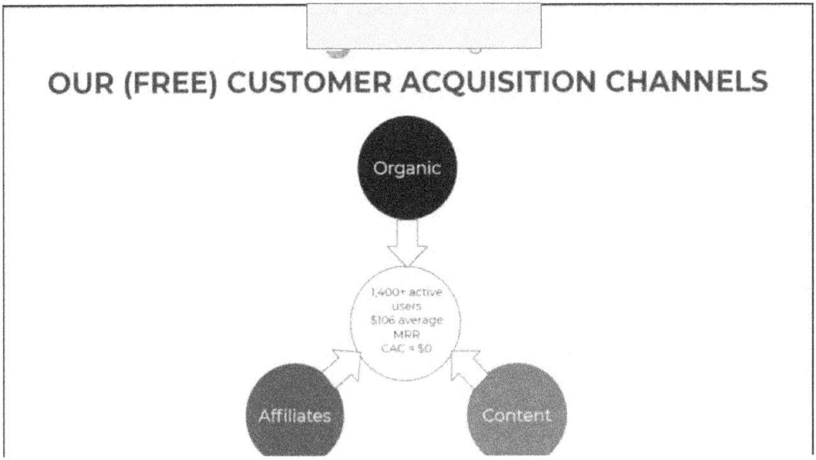
OUR (FREE) CUSTOMER ACQUISITION CHANNELS
Organic
1,400+ active users
$106 average MRR
CAC = $0
Affiliates
Content

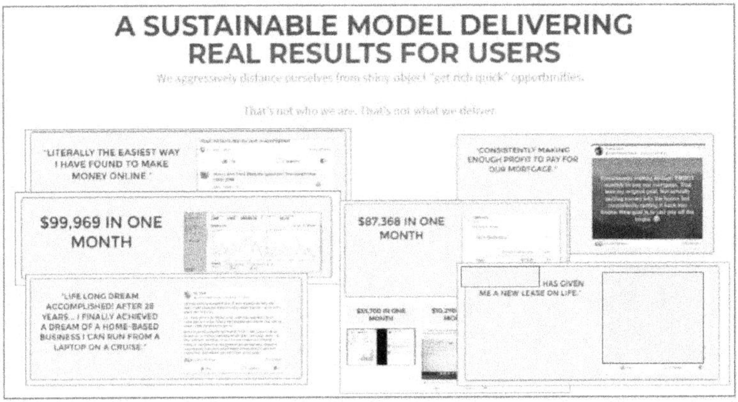
A SUSTAINABLE MODEL DELIVERING REAL RESULTS FOR USERS
We aggressively distance ourselves from shiny object "get rich quick" opportunities.
That's not who we are. That's not what we deliver.
"LITERALLY THE EASIEST WAY I HAVE FOUND TO MAKE MONEY ONLINE."
"CONSISTENTLY MAKING ENOUGH PROFIT TO PAY FOR OUR MORTGAGE."
$99,969 IN ONE MONTH
$87,368 IN ONE MONTH
"LIFE LONG DREAM ACCOMPLISHED! AFTER 28 YEARS... I FINALLY ACHIEVED A DREAM OF A HOME-BASED BUSINESS I CAN RUN FROM A LAPTOP ON A CRUISE."
HAS GIVEN ME A NEW LEASE ON LIFE."

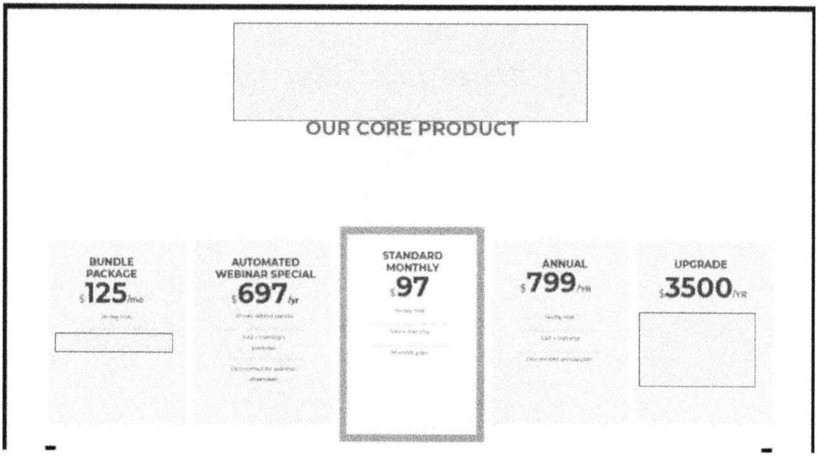
OUR CORE PRODUCT
BUNDLE PACKAGE
$125/mo
AUTOMATED WEBINAR SPECIAL
$697/yr
STANDARD MONTHLY
$97
ANNUAL
$799/YR
UPGRADE
$3500/YR

This Is Where I Told My Team I Was Selling The Business

I don't know where conventional wisdom stands on letting your employees know you're selling, but I'll tell you what I did and why.

Immediately upon the completion of my deck, I let everyone who worked for me (all two of them) know the business was going up for sale. I told them early for two reasons:

1. **Their input impacted the outcome.** I was willing to make a sale contingent on the buyer keeping them on as employees, if keeping their job was important to them. Of course it wasn't, I needed to know now to avoid unnecessary contingencies.
2. **Their participation impacted the outcome.** A sale could be contingent on the developer being available to train new developers. And knowledge transfer from my support person could also be crucial. So I wanted an early commitment they were willing to stay through the transition. (My support person wanted to keep her role, my developer did not. Both generously agreed to assist in the transition).

There may be perils in sharing an intent to sell with your employees, especially with a larger team. And especially if you aren't guaranteeing continuity of employment on the other side.

In my case, I'd known my developer for 20 years, and he

was more friend than employee. And my support person was awesome and always went above and beyond. Both deserved full transparency.

Finding An M&A Broker

That's "merger and acquisitions," if you're as clueless as I was when I began this process.

This is where it gets real.

The role of the broker, as should be obvious, is to find you a buyer. They use their contacts and distribution channels to get you in front of people who acquire companies, as well as representing and advising you through the process.

For any business with substantial value, a broker should be considered mandatory. Brokers will not only have access to buyers, they will advocate for you on valuation, package your business for a sale better than you ever can, legitimize you as a serious seller in the eyes of buyers, identify ways to increase the value of your business, and more. Mandatory.

Alternately, there are platforms that connect sellers to buyers directly (MicroAcquire is the big one as of the time I'm writing this). You'll save on broker commissions, but an M&A broker should pay for themselves, Additionally, they are insurance against all the things that can go wrong.

To find a broker, my entire research strategy was to search X (then Twitter). Utilize various search terms (like "acquired + SaaS", "M&A + SaaS," "SaaS + broker," etc.) From there, I created a spreadsheet mapping out the entire landscape of individuals and firms who could sell my SaaS business. When complete, I had about 25 brokers.

If it's not clear at this point, I had almost no "professional network" to call on. Despite being neck deep in the business for six years and attending 20+ conferences, I knew no one in my position, nor anyone who had ever been in my position. So I had no one to call for guidance on how to proceed.

Despite this, somehow I managed to get an email intro to Thomas Smale, the founder of FE International. They were at the top of my spreadsheet, and as far as I could tell, are the biggest player in the M&A space for businesses my size. He got me on a call with one of his sales people immediately.

The call was fine, and the person I spoke with was enthusiastic and friendly. But when it was over, I was just short of enthusiastic about proceeding. What I was looking for more probing into the specifics of my business, a sense they understood it, and examples of FE International's recent deals for companies that resembled mine.

I won't advise you to make a decision based on rapport or "vibes" here, because I can't be confident I made the correct choice. But I decided to pass on FE International.

So I emailed my deck to the next broker on my list (forget

their name), and my phone was ringing almost immediately. This one was more personal. The enthusiasm was there. Then the subject turned to my monthly churn rate.

"Sorry, we don't ever work with companies with this kind of churn."

<end call>

The tone had turned from enthusiasm to borderline-hostility so quickly that, for the first time, I realized I might have a serious problem. That maybe running an extremely profitable business wasn't enough. That my churn rate might make the business universally toxic and impossible to sell.

(I would later learn my churn was not only very average for my market, I had miscalculated it completely. More on both later.)

Every rejection is closer to a "yes," so I kept going.

Next was a more "boutique" firm, but was spoken highly of by several SaaS founders on X. And the founder was on *Shark Tank* once. So that was cool.

Again, I was on a call with the founder almost as soon as my deck hit their inbox. This call was the one I'd wanted to have. He took the time to ask questions about the business. We got into my numbers. And so on.

In return, I was there to screen him. Here were a few questions I asked:

- What percentage of businesses do you sell?
- How do you market the sale of your companies?
- What resources can you offer?
- What can we do in advance to get the value up?
- What businesses like mine have you sold recently?

On the last question, he just about closed the deal when he told me he'd just helped a solo founder with numbers very similar to mine sell for an eight-figure amount. I'd held off on anchoring myself to any valuation, but the potential for an eight-figure exit hadn't crossed my mind.

Altogether, a great salesman (he'd gotten the deal on *Shark Tank*, after all) and I told him to send over a contract.

Did I rush this decision? From a distance, all the M&A brokers looked the same. So my decision making process was simple:

- Is this a broker with positive, credible, non-bot social media chatter?
- Is this a broker who handles SaaS acquisitions for companies in my revenue range?
- Do they pass the vibe check?

Maybe it was rushed. But in the absence of any decision making formula or reference points, I went for it.

In any case, I had a broker.

Crafting A Business Summary

Shark Tank Guy and his team put me to work immediately.

They sent a long interview with exactly 125 questions. This interview would be used to compile a business summary PDF—the first thing potential buyers would see. What my pitch deck was to M&A brokers, this was to buyers.

Some of the questions I was tasked to answer were:

- What are the threats to the business?
- Are there any expenses that you currently carry that a new owner will not incur?
- Is there anything your competitors are doing that you aren't?
- Who are your top 3-5 competitors?
- Describe your typical customer and why they use your product.
- List clear growth paths for a buyer to significantly increase revenues in the next 24 months.
- What is the typical open rate on the emails you send?
- How many new trial signups do you receive each month (on average)?
- How has this changed over time?

And one that stopped me cold:

- Will you allow a buyer to do a background check on you

once you are under LOI?

If you didn't skip the intro to this story, you know why. And this would send the whole process sideways in short time. But we'll come back to that.

As I went through all 125 questions, I confronted something I'd escaped the past six years, that I could escape no more: not knowing *all* my numbers, inside and out. The pitch deck I'd shopped around was the highlight reel, but going forward, I needed to know *everything*.

When completed, the interview was distilled down into a slick 28 page executive summary and financial overview.

Just a couple more steps before putting my business in front of buyers…

The Recorded Interview

Next step was a "get to know the founder" video interview about the more personal side of the business. My background, how the business started, and why I was selling.

This was recorded and edited to send to potential acquirers, together with the business summary.

My strategy through this entire process was to emphasize to potential acquirers how clueless I was, leaving them with the thought: *"If this doofus can doofus his way to $100k a month,* *our Big Business Brains easily 10x this thing."*

This "aw shucks" strategy was also effortless due to its accuracy. The only two aspects of the business I excelled at were copyrighting and selling (mostly on webinars). The rest was ignored, copied, duct-taped, faked, or just done poorly.

I don't think this "man of the people" persona was what Shark Tank Guy wanted. After the interview, he called it "the most honest interview I've ever seen from a founder." I don't think that was a compliment.

Bookkeeping Disaster Relief: Cleaning Up The Financials

Specifically:

- Reconciling my financial records for a sale.
- Creating three years of (accurate) profit and loss statements.

A broker doesn't want to put a business with inaccurate financials in front of buyers. And I didn't even have a bookkeeper. So there was work to do.

I was given direct orders: clean up your books ASAP. Specifically, the last three years. They set me up with their bookkeeping partner who got work right away. Cost: $2,500.

At this point I learned it would be a worthwhile time and money expense even if my financials *were* in order. As mentioned in a previous chapter, there is a way to optimize your books for a sale that is different from how most are organized. For this reason, you will always want an M&A savvy bookkeeper to redo your financial records. There's no such thing as a small benefit when you're dealing with big numbers..

Unfortunately, this process represented a setback. We were ready to go to market immediately. But clearing up my accounting was a non-negotiable that would take at least two weeks.

Getting A Lawyer

While I waited, I did something I really should have done before getting a broker: Retaining a lawyer.

(You should not follow my lead here. Get a lawyer before signing anything—even a contract for a broker).

As I would soon learn, there's so much legal minutiae involved with a sale that it's mandatory to find a lawyer who specializes in, or has experience with, M&A.

The retainer was $10,000.

(By the time the process was over, the total bill was approximately $15,000).

Intoxicated By Big Numbers Untethered To Reality

"I'd like to ask for $8 million."

This was the first time Shark Tank Guy addressed the subject of valuation.

$8 million was significantly more than I'd expected. This was also before he'd looked under the hood of the business. As such, it would be the last time I ever heard the $8 million figure.

As the weeks progressed, my valuation took a beating. For many reasons I will explain shortly.

The last time any specific numbers were uttered, they were down in the $5 to $6 million range.

Finally, the valuation would be updated to "lets just see what the market tells us."

Now that we are on the serious subject of valuation, let's detour and cover everything that brought my valuation down from its original $8 million estimate.

For many founders, this may be the most important part.

ACT FIVE

THE VALUATION

"Things That Only Go Down" – A Brief History Of My SaaS Business Valuation

As the weeks progressed, and more and more defects of my business were uncovered, my tentative $8 million valuation took a dive (to a huge degree).

By the time we had an LOI on the table (see next chapter), my business was valued at roughly half that initial estimate. This wasn't a big surprise.

Here is the full list of defects that, cumulatively, cost me multiple seven figures:

- 40% of revenue came from one event, one day a year.
- Being "guru lead."
- Being in a weird niche perceived as a fad.
- Declining traffic and revenue.
- Losing my Stripe account.
- The perception of bad churn.

Let's go through each of these. And while none may be relevant to you personally, all will be instructive.

Valuation Liability #1: 40% of revenue coming from one event, one day a year

For the two years prior to the sale, I had one huge promotion in November. This wasn't just a "promotion," I rolled it out like an *event.* I drum-rolled it for six weeks in advance. After which I announced a new product or upgraded version of the software. I limited the number of spots to two or three hundred. I sold spots for four figures. I made it available on a live webinar only. And I did approx. $800,000 in sales two years in a row—on one day, on a single live webinar.

Any prospective acquirer would look at this outrageous revenue spike on a single day (in fact, a single hour) and question if these promotions should factor into valuation at all. They would likely have no confidence they could reproduce my results. In fact, I didn't even have confidence in my own ability—I was out of ideas for new products or upgrades to release in subsequent years, and didn't expect year three to come close to the previous two. So this $800,000 revenue was essentially wiped from the calculus. Instead of valuing based on EBITA, it was EBITAW (webinars).

Had I been able to confidently sell buyers on these promotions being replicable, it would have had a seven figure impact on valuation. But this valuation dent wasn't one I could feel bad about, because I never saw this revenue as repeatable.

And, the combined $1.5m from both years went right into my pocket. The first one had even paid for my first house. So I shed no tears over this one.

Valuation Liability #2: Being "guru lead"

In the first proposal we received (covered shortly) this was mentioned explicitly. When your face is on everything, and everyone associates the business with an individual, then buyers have rightful concerns about what will happen to the business when that "face" is removed.

This is another one I don't regret at all. The personal connection I built with my users was the reason my customer LTV was over $1,000—despite some pretty alarming churn. A lot of founders say they regret being the face of their business because when it comes time to sell, it presents a challenge. I am not among those founders. It cost me at the end, but made me a lot of money along the way.

Valuation Liability #3: Declining traffic and users

While revenue was up, the number of paying users and organic traffic were both down about 8%. Not precipitous, but not good.

This one doesn't need explaining. Rising tides are better than sinking ships.

Valuation Liability #4: I was banned from Stripe

Six months before going up for sale, Stripe suspended my account. (If you don't know what Stripe is, it's how almost everyone processes payments).

Getting banned by your payment processor is a very bad look. It suggests nothing good, and probably something shady. And as expected, I would eventually have a prospective buyer who was nervous, asked questions, and wanted answers. And the answers don't make it sound any less shady, but here it goes…

Earlier I mentioned an annual promotion where I did approximately $800k in sales a day, two years in a row. After the second year's promotion, I received eight $3,500 chargebacks in quick succession, tripped over some Stripe limit on chargebacks, and they banned me.

My $3,500 product was amazing, and promoted accurately. The difference this time was that because spots were limited to 297, I told everyone that "I changed my mind" was not a valid refund reason. You were taking a spot from someone else, I said. So if they had any uncertainty, they should not sign up. It wasn't a "no refund" policy, but I did put them through a *"is your buyer's remorse my fault, or yours?"* quiz before issuing refunds.

Anyway, eight people filed chargebacks. And I said goodbye to my Stripe account (we were unable to take payments for five weeks while we transitioned to Braintree).

This subject would soon take up a big part of a call with a buyer. During which, I was unsuccessful at reducing their suspicion that I was a scam founder running a scam business.

I would have the same concern.

The solution I proposed (which I thought was pretty smart) was to create a document with screenshots of the entire email conversation with all eight users who filed chargebacks, from first to last. This way, the buyer could get full transparency into what led up to the chargeback, and if basic buyers remorse was responsible, or my product was flawed.

The emails vindicated the product, and successfully alleviated their concerns.

Very unlikely many founders will find themselves in precisely this situation, but this is an example of how weird and creative solutions can save a deal.

Valuation Liability #5: "Bad" churn

What follows is the story of a seven-figure mistake.

My monthly churn was the biggest red flag in the whole business. As it turns out, not only was my churn consistent with other SaaS tools in my market, I had calculated it completely wrong. But we're jumping ahead…

Going into the sale process, I had been indoctrinated with the same (fake) info in the SaaS space around standards for "good" churn and "bad" churn. Anything above 5% monthly churn, they say, is "bad" and a huge red flag.

In reality, churn is hugely market dependent. But like an idiot, I bought into the "facts" from these "experts," and had a lot of insecurity around why my churn was so high compared to what's "normal."

According to Stripe, my monthly churn hovered around 12%. This, the "experts" said, was so far into the red flag zone that it could only be explained by deceptive marketing, a terrible product, or every new user clicking the sign up button and having their home immediately firebombed. North of 10%, the "experts" said, and you were a toxic scam artist baby killer.

(Turns out, my churn was never 12%. But we'll get to that in a minute.)

As I saw it, my churn was high for three reasons:

1. My market was very fickle with high turnover. Without going into specifics, my SaaS catered to people who wanted a side hustle, specifically tied to an established ecommerce platform. Seller turnover on this platform was high, and consequently, so was turnover with my SaaS.
2. My SaaS had a steep learning curve. The tool itself was simple, but the business model it facilitated required effort to learn. I made huge improvements to onboarding and training to reduce this burden, but ultimately we had a ton of users who wanted something they could get off the ground and be making money with in a few days. That's just not what we were.
3. We attracted many "get rich quick" users. These users

> quickly learned that's not what my SaaS offered. It's fair to say that the users you attract are always the founder's responsibility, and always a marketing and branding problem. And it's possible I could have done more to dissuade users seeking to "get rich quick." While I was always explicit about what my tool was, and wasn't, our biggest competitor used the opposite messaging. They did promise "pushbutton money riches" (not an exact quote), and we inherited many of their former and prospective users.

You can imagine how few buyers want to sit through a three paragraph pitch about why 12% monthly churn actually isn't "that bad."

In the first call I had with a prospective broker (covered earlier), the call abruptly ended when we got to my churn.

In my first call with the broker I did sign with, he said, "I just want you to know, your 12% churn is a concern for me, and it's going to be a concern for buyers." Great.

When we first put my pitch deck in front of buyers, we polled everyone who turned us down. Churn and not wanting to get involved with a "make money online" business were cited as the two reasons for disinterest.

And of course, when we finally had an LOI, churn was cited as a major reason for the low valuation.

It wasn't until after the sale that I realized my mistake—a

mistake I believe cost me seven figures.

Stripe's churn figure of 12% didn't sit right with me. To get a second opinion, I signed up for a paid SaaS analytics tool. The churn number they gave was lower, but not by much. After the second opinion, I had to conclude the churn was what it was, and put the lower figure in my pitch deck.

Much later, after the sale closed, someone from the new buyer's team referenced my (now their) churn as being 8%. I thought they just misspoke, but this inspired me to revisit my original figure. And what I learned gave me heart palpitations.

That 12% figure, when I dug deeper into the analytics, combined *voluntary* and *involuntary* churn. Voluntary is when users proactively cancel. Involuntary is when their card charge fails. The latter is (mostly) outside your control. And the former is the only churn figure a buyer cares about.

My voluntary ("real") churn, as it turns out, was 8%. That was the figure that should have been in my deck all along. That was the number that should have been put in front of brokers and buyers.

8% is still high, all the "experts" will tell you. And the number still bothered me, because I know my tool was awesome and delivered incredible results for my users. So I still had low self esteem about it.

But soon after discovering my "12%" mistake, I was on a call with another SaaS founder. We served the exact same market. He had the same number of competitors as I did (four, specifically). But his tool was everything mine wasn't: He sold something that was a necessity—a "must have," not a "nice to have" (like mine). It was a timeless tool for our market, not something sensitive to trends (like mine). And it was extremely simple with almost no learning curve (unlike mine). He was generous in screensharing his analytics account, and his voluntary churn was... 8%.

What I learned was 8% was just the reality of our fickle market. The high turnover was innate to the type of user we served. I hadn't been doing anything wrong. We just occupied a world where 8% monthly churn was normal.

I call this a "seven figure mistake" because It's entirely likely that, had churn been a more reasonable 8%, I would have provoked more offers, inspired a bidding war, and sold for $1m to $3m (or more) above the price I eventually received.

What I learned (besides to not blindly trust a number that impacts the biggest financial transaction of your life) is to totally ignore what SaaS experts tell you about churn. It is market dependent, and "normal" churn for a pool cleaner app will have zero relevance to your crypto arbitrage tool. Talk to others in your market and advocate for yourself if anyone outside of it tells you your churn is toxic.

The lessons here are twofold:

1. Know your real churn rate.
2. Know your market. Don't listen to "experts" who wave numbers around as though they're universally applicable.

Things that should have hurt my valuation but were overlooked

Valuation Risk #1: Inflating revenue last minute

"Inflating" is a strong word. Let's say I "strategically optimized revenue under time constraints."

Between starting on my pitch deck and actually getting it in front of buyers, revenue had trended downwards. Exact numbers are fuzzy, but just before shopping the business around, I was at roughly $90k MRR. And I really wanted to get back to $100k MRR. That's a SaaS milestone (aka a "flex") and, in terms of appeal to a buyer, is significantly more than 10% better than $90k.

So I ran a quick promo to my "canceled users" list, which, over six years, had grown to several thousand. I offered them some cool bonuses in return for signing back up, and I quickly captured an additional $10k in MRR.

It should go without saying that there is no such thing hiding any details of your revenue from buyers. That was never my intent. And even if there *was* a way to hide revenue anomalies, I didn't know how. And If I did, I wouldn't. And neither should you. Everything comes out during Due Diligence.

There was an obvious revenue spike on the far right side of the revenue chart we gave to interested buyers, and I was going to have to answer for it. And I was prepared to.

But, it never came up.

I believe the only reason this received no scrutiny is that the entire history of the business was marked by major downward revenue trends, followed by abrupt rebounds. At least once a year I would do a similar scorched-earth promotion, and this last one was consistent with normal patterns throughout the six-year life of the business.

For most businesses, artificially boosting revenue last-minute probably gives the appearance that you're trying to get something past buyers. Not a good first impression.

Valuation Risk #2: Being very sensitive to the Terms Of Service for a major platform

Earlier I mentioned my failure to invest in the growth of the business. I talked about pulling all profits out of the business and putting the money right in my pocket. This suggests either supreme business stupidity, a lack for faith in the longevity of the business, or both. I was "both."

There were no imminent existential risks to the business. But the one I perceived as most possible was the ecommerce platform our users sold on making a small update to their ToS to prohibit the specific "buy low, sell high" model that our users practiced (sorry for being vague).

I even divulged this concern in the business summary sent to prospective buyers. And it may very well have factored into the lower-than-average EBITDA multiple I ended up receiving. But the buyer never brought it up.

Spoiler: Much later, a totally different, non-ToS change to this ecommerce platform ended up mostly destroying the business model my SaaS facilitated. It was a change I never saw coming, but validated my paranoia. Today, I would hesitate to build a SaaS (or any business) whose existence precariously depended on someone else's ToS. Somewhere there is a graveyard of companies that died prematurely for exactly this reason.

If this describes your current business, there's nothing you can do about it. But if I was a buyer, I would have concerns.

Valuation Risk #3: Not knowing my traffic sources

On a list of embarrassing things, this is most embarrassing. It's been four years, and I still can't look back and laugh at this. But you're welcome to.

For six years, I had no idea where my users came from.

From day one, traffic to my SaaS sales page was mostly organic. There was some affiliate traffic, but that was under 10%.

The other 90+% was a mystery.

I had some theories. And some hard facts. But mostly it was a giant question mark.

If forced to answer, it would go something like this:

"Some users come from affiliates, some come from my blog email list, but mostly they come from prospects Googling competitors and reading about how we're better."

That was all I knew. Or "knew."

I had no Google Tag Manager installed. No paid analytics tools. No onboarding "how did you find us?" poll. Nothing but speculation.

Eventually the subject of customer acquisition channels would come up on a call with a prospect. When I said I didn't know, they exploded. They simply weren't buying it, and felt I was hiding something. But my ignorance was real.

That was an intense few minutes, where I was all-but-openly accused of lying. I don't really blame them, because not knowing how you acquire customers is too stupid to believe.

In the end I gave them access to my Google Analytics account (which I had never looked at) and they pieced together enough info to satisfy them. But the general distrust this caused may have done damage.

In the end, I don't have any evidence this ignorance hurt me. But if "the confused mind says no," the confused mind can also say yes, but to a smaller number.

Valuation Risk #4: Grey hat shenanigans

This will be covered in more detail in the Due Diligence chapter. But one of our add-on tools (a Chrome extension) was gently scraping a small amount of data from a large site—a site that would probably prefer we weren't doing that.

Scraping is pretty universally a Terms of Service violation for any major site. And I had concerns this would frighten potential buyers.

In the end, we were open about the scraping, and it was not a concern to the buyer. But it could have gone very differently.

If you're doing anything that represents risk to a buyer, to the best you can, find a way to make it legally or ToS-friendly before a sale.

Valuation Risk #5: Our code base was insane and totally undocumented

Another one that's covered in more detail in "Due Diligence." But in short, our code base had two issues:

1. It was incredibly large.
2. It was not documented.

A buyer could have looked under the hood and determined that my business presented too great of a technical burden, and too great a risk.

In the end, this also was not a concern for the buyer. It also could have gone differently.

The takeaway here: If you're selling a tech business—document your code base. It could make the difference between a sale and no sale.

ACT SIX

GOING TO MARKET

Judgment day. Time to go live.

Shark Tank Guy had a "first access" list—highly motivated clients who paid extra to get early access, specifically to SaaS businesses. He explained that with businesses as profitable as mine, this list alone should cause a bidding war to ensue, and he expected an acquisition would be finalized quickly.

I sat back and waited for a call.

A day later he called, concerned. From his early access SaaS buyers list, he'd only received three requests for the full business summary packet. And all of them passed. I.e. crickets.

This was, he explained, an unusually low level of interest for a SaaS business with extremely healthy EBITDA.

"Let's give it another day," he said.

A day later, the interest level had not improved. He seemed genuinely perplexed.

So he sent out emails to everyone, asking – "Why did you pass?"

Most or all responded with the same two things:

1. The churn was alarming.
2. Some variation of "we think this business is a fad and doesn't have longevity."

The latter was interpreted as a simpler way of saying "We don't understand the money making practice this tool facilitates, but it sounds gimmicky or trend-based, and because of that, we perceive risk."

Remember what I said earlier: "The confused mind always says no."

As a reader, understanding this concern will be a challenge without knowing exactly what the tool was and what niche I was in (see my "disclaimers" section). But suffice to say it was a tool marketed to people who wanted to make money online

I was developing a sense that, from an acquisition perspective, anything in range of *"get rich quick with this weird money glitch!"* aroused suspicion. That wasn't how I marketed my tool, and that's not what it was. It was a serious arbitrage tool with a serious learning curve that delivered real results for my users. But there's a lot of bad products and outright scams in the "selling money" space. And I was, apparently, guilty by association.

As I learned later, two direct competitors faced similar challenges when trying to sell. Both had 3x to 4x my revenue. One (with significantly lower churn) was on the market for seven months before going under LOI. The other never found a buyer at all.

This is where the official valuation dropped to—in the expert eyes of Shark Tank Guy—"I have no idea." (not an exact quote.)

I think he was more disappointed than I was. For me, having been destitute for ¾ of my adult life, most multiple-seven-figure sums roughly translated to the same thing: "I never have to work again." I had taken enough profits up to this point that almost any big number would get me to my target—that aforementioned "2.5% rule" figure (aka "exit number") that buffered me against the threat of doing any compulsory labor ever again. Any buyer willing to pay a non-insulting amount would get me to my Number.

But we didn't even have one of those.

A shark tank of one

After a few days of crickets, he announced he'd received an inquiry from an interested party. A roll-up company that was acquiring SaaS businesses in my space. They reviewed my packet and wanted to talk.

We had a call with two of their execs. The conversation was on the non-quantative side of the business: How I started it, what outcome users came to us for, what makes my product different, what participation level I was comfortable with after a sale, and so on. Mostly I was impressed with the President's story of an innovative technique he'd used to sneak into dozens of Phish concerts 20 years prior. I owed my business to gatecrashing (see Chapter One), so you could call this a "culture fit."

They were a "roll up company." These form when a messy and fragmented space is identified, where there are many players serving a lucrative market. There are "roll up" companies for everything from car washes to campgrounds to mini-golf. They buy up key players in a space, bring everything under one roof to increase efficiency, standardize operations, and create something greater than the sum of its parts.

At this time, there were two roll up companies buying up SaaS tools in my product category. And the other had just purchased a competitor.

Without revealing specifics of our call, here are typical questions a buyer may have on your initial call, that are not addressed by your business summary:

- Why are you selling?
- Biggest competitors?
- Can you elaborate on your growth plan?
- What do you do every day?
- Are you willing to stay with the business?
- How can you explain <weird revenue anomalies>?

This was a two-way screening process, and I had questions for them.

- What experience did they have in the space? (As it turns

out, none).
- What other businesses have they acquired?
- What growth have their acquisitions seen?
- What are their typical expectations of founders after close?

Too early to get into valuation, terms, and deal structure. But I wanted some sense I wasn't walking into a trap.

The next day, Shark Tank Guy calls. They sent a proposal.

My first (maybe only) proposal (aka "Indication of Interest")

The proposal, it was explained, was the last step before a Letter of Intent (where you're legally locked in). It offered a high-level view of deal structure, valuation range, argument supporting the valuation, timeline to close, and post-close expectations.

I asked Shark Tank Guy—who had been increasingly exposed to all the weird defects in my business—if he felt their valuation was reasonable. He felt it wasn't great, but maybe not unreasonable. Given the lack of interest so far, he said, it was in range of what I should expect.

The proposal was informal, without signatures involved, and outlined key terms any LOI would later put a finer point on.

The proposal was also the first glimpse into how my business was viewed from the acquirer perspective. Getting this first outside perspective on something I'd built in solitude for six years was fascinating.

A few highlights from their proposal:

- According to them, the Make Money niche traditionally receives 1-2x EBITDA multiple.
- They also credited my SaaS as being something more sophisticated than a "make money" tool, and that I deserve a higher multiple. But not as high as more standard SaaS multiples.
- According to them, a close competitor recently sold for roughly 2x revenue and 3.5x EBITDA. I was very familiar with this competitor, but this was the first I was learning details of their selling price.
- That competitor was also on the market for seven months before going under LOI.
- They identified risks with my tool that didn't exist with this competitor (specifically lumpier revenue and higher churn).
- They valued my business at a somewhat lower EBITDA multiple than this competitor.
- They promised to close within 30 days.

Shark Tank Guy agreed with most of their points, but felt they were underselling the value. He expressed an interest in pushing back a little on valuation, but in light of the low interest this far, he felt it was in range of "fair."

Selling when you only have one offer is a very bad idea

Let's take a detour to cover what I did at this stage, and why you (probably) shouldn't do the same.

Every single piece of literature I'd read on selling your business said the same thing:

Always get multiple offers.

Multiple parties bidding off each other drives up the price. Never take the first offer that comes, they say.

If I agreed with the proposal, the next step was a Letter of Intent. The LOI would be a legally binding contract where the business would come off the market, and both parties agreed to advance to a sale pending the settling of various contract minutiae. Like a marriage that is still in the annulment window.

If I signed an LOI, the potential for any additional offers ceased. And I would be committing to a significantly lower EBITDA multiple than was normal for SaaS.

And yet, it ensured enough money to comfortably live off of forever. Which was my big "why" behind the last six years.

Alternately, I could hold out for more offers. Which brought the risk of the existing offer coming off the table. And if no better offers came in—or no more offers at all—I would regret it forever.

Then again, we hadn't yet made the business "public." My business listing hadn't traveled further than the broker's "early access" SaaS buyer list. So it was only crickets from the (very) small portion of the market who had seen my listing.

This was the highest stakes *"bird in hand..."* decision I had never made.

Shark Tank Guy wasn't saying this outright, but I didn't sense optimism over taking my chances on the open market. My sense was that if a business like mine was going to find a buyer on the public marketplace, there would be at least measurable interest from the early bird list.

The market was speaking, albeit not yet at full volume. But its whispers weren't good.

Then again, taking the first offer, as I saw it, only made sense at the intersection of two factors:

1. A serious time constraint: circumstances that required you to sell, fast.
2. A business so toxic that another buyer wasn't likely to surface in a timely manner.

Short of this, you're simply leaving tons of money on the table.

Every minute I spent meditating on this, I changed my mind at least four times.

Finally, I made a decision. Influenced by two factors:

1. **The time constraint.** My developer—whose participation in any transition was indispensable and (probably) not negotiable for any buyer—was on his way out. He was expressly not thrilled about delaying the next phase of his life so someone else could have their big payday. He'd been incredibly supportive from day one, but asking him to hang on while the business potentially sat on the market for months was not only unfair, it probably wasn't an option. I was running out of time.
2. **Competitor feedback.** My biggest competitor had spent seven months on the market before finding a buyer. They had stronger metrics all around, and even then, their EBITDA multiple wasn't great. While this was anecdotal, it nudged my expectations towards something closer to reality. The world was not clamoring to buy my kind of business.

We gave the green light to send over an LOI.

ACT SEVEN

THE CLOSE

The Letter Of Intent

The timeline from proposal to Letter of Intent was 24 hours.

This was also called an "LOI" or "term sheet." I wasn't committed until I signed it.

The LOI is a prospective buyer saying "Here's what we'll pay you for your business, and here are the terms, pending nothing weird turns up during Due Diligence."

This contract also put a finer point on the valuation and some of the terms hinted at in the Proposal.

The deal structure was not a straight cash deal. It was significantly more complicated.

The majority would be paid in cash (paid out over several months as various commitments were met).

A smaller percentage would be paid in common stock, paid out after two years and valued as a multiple of EBITDA.

An even smaller percentage was an "earnout." This is a payment contingent on hitting certain revenue milestones over the coming months. This was to secure my near-term motivation to help grow the business.

They were going to take my SaaS to the moon, my broker said. They had a team of ten in place to do everything my team of two couldn't. They were going to build an army of affiliates, churn out tons of content, set up booths at industry events, run paid ads, and dominate the space.

Short of total negligence, I had little concern a team their size could exceed the revenue target needed to achieve my earnout.

And if their team was even barely competent, the 20% as stock would convert to millions more—a second payday that could possibly be bigger than the first.

Yet both of these "probably's" were out of my control.

So I put the same question to both my broker and my lawyer:

What if they assume ownership and just completely fumble it? What protections do I have if they do everything wrong and run the business into the ground?

The answer from both was the same: None. No guarantees, no protection.

Shark Tank Guy was more optimistic (*"This is a great team and they're really going to take over this market."*)

My lawyer, less so (*"It's not uncommon that earnouts don't earn out and stock goes to zero."*)

As the LOI burned a hole in my inbox, I knew the decision came down to one question:

Could I live with an outcome where the upfront cash was the only payment I ever received? Was that number alone enough to live with, without regret?

To answer this, I returned to my aforementioned "Exit Number." The liquid net worth figure that, if I cashed out 2.5% per year, I could live well and never run out of money.

I did the napkin math on taxes, a "thank you" payment to my developer, giving the broker his cut.... The cash payment *should* put me just over my Exit Number.

I signed the LOI. Let's go.

My dual identity, unmasked

Just before the Due Diligence ended, things went sideways.

Astute readers will remember two details from earlier in this tale:

1. I am a convicted "eco-terrorist" (with the colorful Google footprint that suggests).
2. For that reason, I used a pseudonym for anything public-facing.

My felon-shame-level was zero, but you never know what other people will think.

There was never an intent to conceal my identity. But I never saw a need to get in front of it either. My crimes were not profit-driven, involved no deception or fraud or anything relevant in a business context, and were over 20 years old.

When I signed the "letter of intent," it was the first time the buyer had seen my legal name.

Within hours, I got a call from my broker.

"They Googled you."

"What's the damage?" I asked.

"They're nervous. I'll see what I can do."

<Calls back an hour later>

"Get this: someone on their executive team is a vegan. They understood your….crimes. And put the executive team at ease. Deal is on."

Due Diligence

The Due Diligence phase began immediately.

DD is throwing open the front door, back door, trap door, junk drawer, skeleton closet, and every other access point to every part of your business, so the buyer can confirm there are no surprises, and that you've represented everything accurately. Everything from your payment processor, to your tax returns, to your customer support inbox gets audited. And all the secrets of your business are laid bare.

They are looking for lies, trouble, and risk. And if they find any of those, your valuation—or the deal itself—are in jeopardy.

By this point I had read several DD horror stories. Buyers looking for excuses to negotiate down the value. Finding weird personal emails in the business inbox and getting spooked. Uncovering benign non-skeletons incorrectly interpreted as risk—things which never occurred to the seller to divulge—and calling off the deal.

From the beginning, my strategy was to be upfront that my business was a mess. So their expectations were low.

As DD progressed, everything seemed to fall into four categories (with some overlap between each):

1. General DD
2. Legal DD
3. Financial DD
4. Technical DD

They sent a list with over a dozen categories of files to submit, and a list of accounts they needed guest access to. Without revealing the specifics of their DD formula, here's what a thorough DD might require:

General DD can include things like:

- Corporate bylaws
- List of all business assets
- Employee records and contracts
- Employee compensation records
- Employee benefit records
- List of vendors
- List of recurring subscriptions required to operate
- List of all intellectual property owned by the business
- Creating demo accounts to test the software

Legal DD can include things like:

- Articles of incorporation
- Correspondence with governments pertaining to your business
- Licenses or permits needed to operate the business
- Federal or local tax correspondence: audits, notices, etc
- Non-compete agreements
- Non-disclosure agreements
- Description of all oral agreements
- All contracts with contractors, customers or vendors
- All litigation or legal records

Financial DD can include things like:

- Anyone who owns a stake in the business and accompa-

nying shareholder agreements, stock certificates, etc
- Any debt, liens, mortgages, etc held by the business
- Loan documents
- Three to five years of financials (balance sheets, profit and loss statements, etc)
- Bank statements
- Payment processor access
- Three to five years of tax returns

Technical DD can include things like:

- A system map (high level visual of the code base with all the components and how they interact)
- Access to the code base

Both my broker and lawyer gave the same stern directive:

"Don't hide anything."

It's all going to come out.

My first mistake was interpreting "don't hide anything" too literally. And I was punished for this quickly. **No one warned me that oversharing is also a mistake.**

This lesson first came when asked to provide "all" correspondence with government agencies about the business. I thought I was being a spirited, obedient, and dutiful team player by sending over a random notice from the state of Nevada which (incorrectly) claimed a few hundred dollars in unpaid payroll taxes. The notice was insignificant, pertained to a long-since-departed employee, and was rightfully ignored. But the buyer's team interpreted it as some kind of big pending legal matter and set off a long chain of crisis-level emails insisting I resolve this before the deal could proceed.

This lesson came again soon after, when asked to divulge any "complaints against your business" (or something like that). In an attempt to err on the side of transparency, I requested clarification on "complaints," since most customer service inbox emails could technically be considered "complaints" (our inbox was 30,000 emails deep, and no user was emailing us for fun). This set off another mini-crisis email chain about my "30,000 customer complaints." It required a whole Zoom call to resolve.

A different lesson took the form of a last minute panic over discrepancies surrounding the legal name of my businesses. The IRS had the name spelled as one word, the Secretary of State article incorporation had the same name but separated as two. And their lawyers needed me to scramble to align everything before they would approve the sale.

The most time consuming part (for me) was the "asset list." When you're running a business, you don't think of it as a collection of "assets." It's a symphony of enterprise that pumps money into your bank every month, not an assembly of parts. But the buyer needed a list of every component. This required a comprehensive spreadsheet with every email list, every social media asset, every part of our tech stack, every piece of intellectual property, every URL, every SOP.... *Everything.*

Due Diligence also forced me to do things I should have been doing all along. Like know my operating expenses. One of the benefits of being cash flow positive from day one is that you're under no pressure to know your margins, your total fixed expenses, your average variable expenses, your exact labor costs, etc. Every month money goes out, and a much bigger amount comes back. To me, it was as simple as that.

For the first time, I was compelled to share (and thus, know) exact numbers. So if you wondering what the expense breakdown for a $100,000 a month SaaS business is, I can finally tell you:

- Labor: 14k/month (lead dev, part time contract devs, email support)
- Fixed expenses $6,706/month (everything from AWS to Intercom to error logging tools to website conversion boosting widgets to sales funnel software to email list management tools and lots more. Exactly 24 monthly recurring expenses.)

Financial DD required its own call. They brought on their financial auditor to ask me questions, all oriented towards preparing him for his audit. He spent several days tearing through my payment processor records, Quickbooks, and bank statements looking for discrepancies or suspicious anomalies. After a week, everything came back clean.

The final stage of DD was the only one I had serious concerns about: Technical Due Diligence.

The purpose is to audit everything on the technical side and answer questions like: Is the code base documented? (It wasn't). Is there more than one developer who knows the code base? (there wasn't). Can it scale without a full rewrite? (IDK).

They scheduled a call with their lead dev and my lead dev for a Thursday.

I had two serious concerns I felt could derail the sale.

Existential Threat #1: Gray hat shenanigans

So far I've been referring to the business as "my SaaS" for the sake of simplicity, but it was in fact a suite of seven tools: One web app, and six chrome extensions. The second-highest revenue generating tool (a Chrome extension) relied on web-scraping to work its magic. Disallowing scraping is boilerplate ToS for any website. We were almost definitely not ToS-compliant with the site we scraped. I had concerns that anything "gray hat" would make the entire business toxic to a buyer.

So the day before the technical DD call, I had a meeting with my developer. We needed a plan to address how to handle this if and when scraping came up during Due Diligence.

Maybe, I hoped, he would tell me there are tiers to scraping, and we were on the non-offensive end. Maybe he could explain how our scraping methodology wasn't "real" scraping, and something more ToS-friendly.

His response, in short, was: "Scraping is scraping. And we're scraping."

We'd have to face this one head on. Whatever happened, happened.

Existential Threat #2: Large, unwieldy, undocumented code base

As a non-tech founder, this part was over my head. But my developer explained that our code base was extremely complex, extremely large, extremely undocumented, and would be extremely difficult to navigate for any new devs.

Any purchase agreement would involve a small window of time in which the old developer would be available to assist new developers in the transition (I was told 30 to 90 days was typical).

When the buyer's lead dev received access to the code base, it could be immediately evident that more than 30, 60, or 90 days would be required to untangle everything. And that could spook them out of closing (or inspire them to require my developer to commit to being involved longer than he was willing, which would sabotage the sale just the same).

My developer said documenting the code base at this point

wasn't realistic, and we just had to roll with it.

Both of these concerns made the technical due diligence call the most tense phase.

The call was on a Thursday. My developer called me immediately after to give the full report. I cut right to my two concerns.

"What did they say about our data scraping?"

He told me their developer asked him to explain our "data collection methodology" which he did without volunteering the word "scraping."

"So you're scraping?" their developer asked.

"Yes." my developer said.

And they changed the subject.

Bullet #1 dodged.

"What did they say about the size and complexity of our code base?"

He said this never came up.

Bullet #2 dodged.

The entire technical DD call, he explained, was short, the scrutiny minimal, it was his sense their developer was in far over his head, and didn't understand anything he was looking at.

(It's also just as likely their developer understood exactly what he was looking at, knew he had a skilled team under him, and was fully able and willing to untangle and document the code base himself. Our role was to make everything available, transparent, and answer all questions. We fulfilled that.)

My developer's exact quote summarizing the whole call was: "I've faced tougher questions checking into a hotel."

That concluded Due Diligence. Nothing dealbreaking turned up, and they were ready to proceed.

The entire process took 25 days.

Escrow

This is a separate document to sign which specifies the escrow agent to be used, and the payment schedule.

If there's any differences between escrow agents besides price, I am unaware. My broker recommended one and we went with them. The cost was $1,000.

At this point, we were 40 days from the original proposal. This was the final phase before riches or ruin.

Asset Purchase Agreement

The APA covers all terms of the sale in one 32 page contract. This is the Big One: everything that's been discussed—and a few that haven't—translated into thick legalese.

This immediately goes to your lawyer, and the back-and-forth red-lining begins.

90% of the discussions from this point were between lawyers discussing lawyer things. Why does the language read this way instead of this other way? Why did you add this line that makes my client a legal party to the terms of service for entities he has no involvement with? The consulting agreement should not be a separate document. What if an asset is non-transferable (like PayPal accounts)? And so on.

The process lasted weeks, in a cycle that went like this:

1. The lawyer sends changes for your approval.
2. The lawyer sends the founder-approved document to their lawyer.
3. Their lawyer approves, rejects, or sends compromise edits back.
4. When there's an impasse, a call is had.
5. Repeat.

And there were many calls.

Among the most contested items:

Debating the earnout payment. The APA had this as a flat percentage of revenue for the remainder of the year. We felt there should be a "floor" to this payment, to protect against the business being mishandled or abandoned and revenue going to zero. This was hotly debated.

Debating my developer's obligations. Securing the assistance of technical talent through a transition is normal and reasonable. However the original APA didn't put a cap on his time commitment. This left open the potential for unreasonable demands, him being unwilling to meet these demands, which in turn would leave me in breach of contract. Over time, we were able to negotiate his time commitment down to an amount everyone could agree to.

Debating the non-compete. The non-compete language was vague enough that by one interpretation, I was prevented from doing any business in the niche my software occupied. The spirit of the non-compete was to prevent me launching a *directly* competitive tool, but the language did not reflect that. We argued that allowing me to continue operating in the space was beneficial for their business—since I still had a stock interest in my SaaS, me remaining active in the market and continuing to build an audience was of mutual benefit. After much discussion, the language was clarified.

Debating my time commitment long-term. They made clear they were unwilling to acquire any company without securing the long-term participation of the founder. No surprise there.

And my stock interest all but ensured my ongoing participation anyway. But they also needed this commitment in writing. As with my developer, there was no cap on my time commitment. Much discussion followed around defining my time obligation, to prevent permanent indentured servitude.

I had been unprepared for the sheer volume of small details with big impacts that had to be resolved—each one potentially carrying seven-figure implications.

And there was one that almost cost me the sale…

Where I almost lost the sale: Part three (four? five? I lost count)

I'd dodged the technical due diligence bullet. I'd dodged the "they Googled you" bullet. But what happened next was the closest the deal came to truly falling apart.

As the last of the APA's finer points were being settled, the buyer abruptly announced they required an additional asset: my blog. This blog had no direct connection to the SaaS tool other than, at one time, being my primary lead generation source. As the blog became less central for acquiring customers, I let it languish. Then Google did a couple big core algorithm updates that sent search engine traffic down to the low-dozens a day. It was a nearly worthless asset.

While the blog was all but dead, I had plans for it. After I sold my existing business, I intended (to the extent that any non-compete allowed) to launch new SaaS tools to the same market. And part of that plan was to resurrect the blog and restore it to its former high-traffic glory.

So when they asked me to throw the blog in as part of the sale (in the later stages of negotiations, I should add), I saw it as robbing me of all future potential to operate in the same market. I told them "no" and dug in my heels. Over the long term, I saw the blog as a seven figure asset. If they wanted to assign value to it as an asset, they could increase their offer price.

My rough quote to them was:

"If it has no value, then you shouldn't want it. And if it does have value, then I need to be paid for it."

We were in a stalemate, and my broker told me they were ready to walk away from the deal. Their zeal came from the results of a site traffic audit, where they identified one article on the blog (of hundreds) that sent traffic to the SaaS sales page. They wanted that traffic.

What's incredible to me now, as I write this four years later, is that I was willing to walk away from the sale over this blog. I was one "yes" away from hitting my "exit number" and securing a payday that would allow me to never work again, but the blog was a hill I was willing to die on.

In the end, they agreed to let me retain ownership on certain conditions that maintained links and traffic to the software. And the sale proceeded.

This near-miss is the reason I emphasized earlier to "know your outcome." I *thought* I had a clarity of purpose. But when faced with something that could derail the sale, I took my eye off the ball. I wasn't fully committed.

Could have ended differently.

Commit to your outcome.

Postscript: I never did resurrect the blog in any meaningful way. Today, the blog still receives organic daily visitor traffic in the low-dozens and is essentially worthless.

Closing

On August 12th, a final draft of the APA hit my inbox.

Six years and one month after launching my weird bootstrapped niche tech business, everything came down to one signature.

Actually, five.

The final Docusign batch looked like this:

1. Asset Purchase Agreement: "The contract."

2. Consulting Agreement: This addresses the seller's obligations to aid in the transition after the sale.
3. Intellectual Property Assignment Agreement: This signs over rights of all IP to the buyer.
4. Assignment and Assumption Agreement: I have no idea what this is, but it was 3 pages.
5. Bill of Sale: Also 3 pages.

Click, click, click, click, and click.

I was free.

ACT EIGHT

THE TRANSITION

After the obligatory round of "welcome to the team" emails, the transition began.

My involvement approached full time hours in the beginning, as I took on the massive undertaking of onboarding their team, granting them access to dozens of business-critical tools and platforms, and knowledge transfer. You don't realize how complicated your business is until you have to teach it to someone else.

The migration was explicitly divided into four categories, and I was assigned a different point of contact for each:

1. Overall coordination: Asset transfer of domains, financial accounts, etc.
2. Marketing migration Asset and knowledge transfer of all marketing assets, email databases, etc.
3. Technical migration: Asset and knowledge transfer of the code repository, staging environments, etc. (This was the part that should have been most urgent to them. While they had access to me indefinitely, they had my developer for a very short window. Incredibly, they only spoke to him once. He received several desperate pleas for help after the end of his obligation, but they missed the window).
4. Personnel migration: Asset and knowledge transfer of customer services inboxes, non-technical operations, etc.

This involved many Zoom calls, and hundreds of emails.

Here's a few calls we had in the early weeks:

- Migration kickoff call
- Marketing call
- Technical call
- Personnel call (The person I had this call with was flabbergasted that I handled almost everything myself. It was a short call.)
- Payment processor call
- Content team call
- Software training call

Also imagine about one million "send me the code" two-factor authentication emails. I lived in my inbox for weeks.

From proposal to APA, our communication had spanned about 150 emails.

From APA to the end of migration, the number was over 500.

The transition never had a "finish line." The dozens of daily emails and texts and calls slowly faded to one or two a day, then one a week. Then the questions stopped coming in completely.

ACT NINE

POST-MORTEM

The final check

Last thing was a thank you check to my developer.

He'd joined the business 18 months in. Was indispensable through the whole journey. Saved the business from ruin multiple times. Stepped up in every emergency. Rode out the entire sale process without any guarantee of a payout. Made almost everything possible. Total legend.

I'd also tapped him from my social circle, and had known him for almost 20 years. We'd go years without talking, but he'd been a constant presence. After drifting off from our nearly identical riff raff lifestyles of legal-homelessness and suburban hunter-gatherer outlaw-lite shenanigans, we reconnected at the exact time that one of us was a developer, and the other running a $40k/month software business whose last developer had just quit.

There's no formula for a parting gift in this exact situation. In the end, I settled on a round six-figure number that—after all taxes and broker fees—amounted to roughly 10% of my sale proceeds.

Other than him, I'd gone through most of the last six years alone. But I paused to consider who else I owed my "success" to, which brought to mind the ex who had floated me in the early stages of my entrepreneurial journey.

Apparently she hadn't forgotten me either—she curiously slid into my inbox shortly after the sale. In the ensuing conversation, a joke was made about me owing her "back rent plus interest." It seemed also appropriate as a non-joke. So I decided to wire her $5,000.

After a long email thread where she provided the info necessary for a transfer—account number, routing number, etc—I hit "send" on the $5k wire.

My last email read "wire sent." She didn't respond.

A(nother) parting joke at my expense

After an adult life of extreme poverty lasting well into my thirties, I was now in the top 2% of liquid net worth (and top one-tenth-of-one-percent for my age).

So I can share one final anecdote. A parting joke that comes at my expense. One I invite you to laugh at and learn from. I seek no sympathy.

Buried in the Purchase Agreement was a paragraph that offered a cash buyout of my stock. This cash payment could be redeemed with a single email if I chose to abandon the stock option before a specific date.

If the business did well, the stock would be worth millions—something well in excess of the buyout amount. So you would only invoke this "cash out early" payment if:

1. You really needed drug money fast, or,
2. You believed the business was going to zero under new ownership.

We'll call this cash amount "a significant multi-six-figure sum." *Very* significant.

Several months after the deal closed, my optimism about the future of the business had diminished. I was not privy to any financials or metrics at that point. I just failed to see the momentum that would give my stock any value. My vibes-based napkin math just didn't pencil out.

When I finally abandoned hope for my stock having value, I was still in the redemption window for this cash buyout. One email, they would wire over this "significant six figure amount," and I was legally divested (and a lot richer). *One email.*

Here's the punchline: I had missed this "stock buyout" paragraph in the contract. Literally didn't know this six-figure sum was an option.

It wasn't obscured through thick legalese. My lawyer hadn't misrepresented this paragraph to me, nor failed to address it (his exact quote over email: "Are you okay with this paragraph?" I didn't respond.) It wasn't even that I failed to read the contract. I just.... missed that paragraph.

One email that would have converted to an extra 20% (approximately) in sale proceeds. And I missed it.

Read your contracts.

Twice.

Post-mortem: What happened to my weird niche bookstrapped SaaS after the sale

I had a lot invested in the growth of the business after the sale, and only some of it was financial. I was proud to have built the rare "make money" tool that actually delivered results. Some of my users had been with me for years, even before I launched the software. People were using my tool to pay rent and put their children through college. For me, improving the product meant the business would grow, which meant a payday down the road that was "nice to have," but it wasn't something I *needed.*

On the other hand, improving the product meant a lot more for my users, many of whom depended on it for their livelihood. I had a very specific road map for growing the business that had been constrained only by my time. And I was excited to guide the product and my users to the next level.

But I wasn't the owner anymore.

It was apparent early we didn't share the same vision for growth, and my roadmap was openly at odds with theirs. So it goes.

After one specific call which starkly highlighted our divergent strategies, I never heard from them again.

The earnout did not materialize.

The value of my stock went to zero.

Shortly after, they sold off the product to another company.

Shortly after, the new owners shut it down completely.

As for me, I lived in hotels for a while. Launched another SaaS business, which got to $10k MRR before a platform change shut it down. Embarked on a series of cringe middle-age YOLO activities (like *you've* never thought about recording an anonymous hip hop album). Started buying random real estate at tax auctions (anyone want to live in an abandoned seafood market, let me know).

As for what's next, the answer is: Everything, *except* getting a job…

At various times, Peter Young has been a fugitive, founder, protester, author, prisoner, felon, spokesperson, entrepreneur, hobo, saboteur, publisher, orator, infiltrator, agitator, investor, and criminal.

By various federal agencies and trade groups, he has been called a terrorist, eco-terrorist, domestic terrorist, "special interest" terrorist, burglar, accessory after the fact, danger to the community, armed and dangerous, flight risk, escape risk, and unindicted co-conspirator.

By various journalists and authors, he has been called arrogant, unrepentant, privileged, notorious, defiant, controversial, self-aggrandizing, entitled, and "basically homeless."

Today he runs internet businesses and continues his lifelong and unbroken succession of conspiracies.

He can be contacted at:
peter@peteryoung.me

ALSO BY PETER YOUNG

www.ingramcontent.com/pod-product-compliance
Lightning Source LLC
Chambersburg PA
CBHW050529240926
51846CB00003B/752
9781957452258